Lost for Words

Also by John Humphrys

The Great Food Gamble
Devil's Advocate

Lost for Words

The Mangling and Manipulating of the English Language

JOHN HUMPHRYS

Hodder & Stoughton

First published in Great Britain in 2004
by Hodder & Stoughton
A division of Hodder Headline

A Hodder & Stoughton book

1 3 5 7 9 10 8 6 4 2

A CIP catalogue record for this title is available from the British Library

Hardback ISBN 0 340 83658 X

Typeset in Sabon by
Rowland Phototypesetting Ltd,
Bury St Edmunds, Suffolk
Printed and bound in Great Britain by Clays Ltd, St Ives plc

Hodder Headline's policy is to use papers that are natural, renewable and
recyclable products and made from wood grown in sustainable forests.
The logging and manufacturing processes are expected to conform to the
environmental regulations of the country of origin.

Hodder and Stoughton Ltd
A division of Hodder Headline
338 Euston Road
London NW1 3BH

*To my grandchildren, struggling to learn to speak,
in the hope that English will be as important to
them as it has been to me.*

Acknowledgements

I am grateful to friends and colleagues who have offered so much help since I began this book, especially Diana Bell, Julian Birkett, Philip Booth, Peter Franklin, Dilip Lakhani, Dave Provis, Andrew Taylor, Digby Jones and Nicholas Spice.

Luigi Bonomi has been his usual supportive self and it has also been a pleasure to work with Rowena Webb and Hazel Orme. If I named all those who have made a contribution, the list would run into several pages. Thousands of people have written to me over the years with their concerns about what is happening to the language and I have raided their letters for examples. I am grateful to all of them. These are not G.K. Chesterton's 'people of England that never have spoken yet'. These are people who do speak – and speak with passion out of love for the language. I am enormously grateful to all of them.

It is my name on the cover of this book, but it would not have happened without John Wakefield. John is friend, inspiration and collaborator. It is his book as much as it is mine.

Contents

Health Warning

Almost everything seems to carry a health warning these days. Smoking kills you and food makes you fat. Too much alcohol makes you drunk and too much sunshine gives you cancer. Books can kill too. When I bought *Animal Farm* nearly fifty years ago I wandered out of the shop reading it and was so absorbed I kept wandering and reading – right across a main road. God knows how the lorry missed me.

This book should, perhaps, carry a health warning for different reasons. Some people will expect it to be an attack on those who have no respect for the English language. And so it is. But their views of good English may differ from mine. Hence the warning. If your blood pressure tends to be on the high side and you believe a book about English should strictly observe every rule of grammar, then be warned: many of those rules will be broken in the following pages, some inadvertently but most in full knowledge of the offence that may be caused.

I do not believe you will find any split infinitives. There is no particular reason for that, except that I happen to find them ugly. You will find many sentences beginning with conjunctions (see the last paragraph) and many ending with a preposition. I shall probably not go as far as the little boy who, it is said, disliked a book about Australia that his mother was fond of reading to him at bedtime and finally demanded, 'What have you brought that book I don't like being read to out of about Down Under up for?'

On the other hand, I sympathise fully with the gauche young man from rural Mississippi who won a scholarship to Harvard. On his first day there he approached a couple of cocky young New England socialites. 'Hey, y'all, where's the library at?' They sniggered among themselves and one replied haughtily, 'At Harvard we prefer not to end a sentence with a preposition.' The young redneck thought for a moment and said, 'Okay. Where's the library at, asshole?'

This book is not a primer. Nor (as if you'd needed telling) is it a scholarly analysis of English. Even if I'd wanted to write one of those I don't exactly have the academic qualifications. The only degrees I have are those honorary ones that universities give people once they have become reasonably well known.

I left school at fifteen with a clutch of O levels

and something much more important: a basic understanding of how to put a sentence together. In those days it was enough to help me get a job on a small newspaper and make a decent living over the years since. Grammar has been good to me.

Nor is this book about style. The Victorian writer Matthew Arnold dismissed those who thought he could teach them style with these words: 'Have something to say and say it as clearly as you can. That is the only secret to style.'

That is what this book is about: saying things clearly. I have several worries on that front.

It worries me that children do not get the same help that I had more than half a century ago. I wish the basic rules of grammar were still taught to every child. They do matter – even though we may make a conscious decision to break them from time to time.

I hate sloppy, overblown, cliché-ridden language when it is used by those who should know better – not least when it is broadcast by the BBC. I hate jargon. I hate the idea – increasingly fashionable in academic circles – that rules confine language. They do not. They liberate it. As George Orwell said, slovenly language 'makes it easier for us to have foolish thoughts'.

In short, I worry about the way language is mangled. But I worry even more about the way it can be manipulated by people trying to sell us things – whether they be double-glazing salesmen or international banks. Or politicians. As Richard Hoggart says, language gives power to all citizens in a free society. But it can do so only if it is used properly.

That is the reason for this book.

CHAPTER ONE

Our Common Language

So just how mega is this then? A book on English. Never really meant to do it. No way. Then I'm like with my *publisher*? She's like yeah, John, everyone gets really uptight about the gash way we speak now. We need something fly, yeah? Like totally awesome? And I'm *so* like no way . . . I'm up to here with stuff? And she's like, tell me about it. But she blags me and we do a deal and I'm cool and she's, like, Bless! Know what I mean?

You probably do know what I meant. It might have been a bit of a struggle but I dare say you will have got the meaning of that hideous paragraph in the end. If you were fifteen years old you'd have had no problem – even though the vocabulary may be outdated already. Teen language changes far too quickly for book deadlines to cope. But children have no difficulty in understanding each other. They have adapted the language to suit themselves. It may not be the English you or I were taught at school, but it works for them.

It proves a number of things. One is that you don't need all the rules to make yourself understood. That single paragraph broke half the rules in the book. There were sentences without verbs and verbs without subjects and punctuation that would have had my old teacher reaching for her smelling-salts – or her cane. The present tense was used when it should have been the past tense and statements were turned into questions with an uplift at the end of the sentence for no earthly reason that I can think of – except that it happens a lot in Australian soaps. But it worked. You probably got the drift.

Grumpy old men like me are appalled by it – partly because it reminds us of how old we are – and so are many others. Yet I suspect it does less damage to the language than this sort of thing:

Each specialist library will be the product of a community of practice of all those interested in knowledge mobilisation and localisation of their domain.

Or this:

We've had over six months of detailed consultation during which the original proposals were amended and that can continue in a proper scrutiny not an attempt to wreck the bill by long-grassing it forever.

Or this:

Cameras had been placed where there was a partnership concern about road safety.

Or this:

The right to be offensive is always a prerequisite for public debate going forwards.

Or this:

It was a victory for terror.

Or this:

Coke Adds Life.

None of those lines was written by fifteen-year-olds talking to each other, deliberately trying to exclude the ancients. They were all written by people in the business of communicating: politicians, advertising copy-writers, journalists, government officials. And they were getting paid to do it – paid a great deal of money in the case of the copy-writers. Sugary fizzy drinks tend to rot your teeth and make you fat – but not in the world of advertising.

How can people speak and write this sort of

rubbish? How can they be so indifferent to the way their words sound? How can broadcasters transmit them and newspapers print them? How is it that the purveyors of the equivalent of junk food are not hauled up before the linguistic equivalent of the Food Standards Agency and forced to forfeit their licence to speak?

Ugly language can ruin your day. I spend my waking hours among words. I am reading the papers when sensible people are still snoring. I sit in a studio listening to my guests (and, often, to my own voice) massacring the English language. I hear politicians use verbal trickery to bamboozle the audience, and 'experts' of all stripes resort to jargon under the smallest amount of pressure. I hear scientists and cultural leaders failing to deliver simple messages and then, having failed, blaming the media for showing no interest in their subjects.

During the day I chair conferences where businessmen nod sagely while gurus spout meaningless platitudes for huge fees. Then I go home and listen to broadcasters doing just what I was doing a few hours ago – sometimes better, sometimes worse.

I love words. Let me be honest, I love the sound of my own voice. Show me a broadcaster who doesn't. I like listening to other people almost as much – especially when they are using good English. Sometimes there is a real thrill of pleasure. It is like walking in the surf, letting the waves lap over your bare feet. Then you step in something nasty. Ugly language is the detritus washed up on a beach. The metaphor is not ideal. Even the most polluted beach will ultimately be cleaned by the waves – unless, of course, more pollution is spilled into the sea and washed up with each new tide.

I have a friend, an English teacher, whose main ambition in life is to inspire her pupils. What she most wants to do is read Keats and Donne with them and explore the language that has so enriched her own life. Instead, she has to spend much of her time dealing with this sort of rubbish:

There is no formal link between the context of the activities and skills triplets targeted. Therefore teachers may match the activities to the skills triplets in whatever way they think appropriate, e.g. a candidate who is 'hot-seated' as a character from a literary text studied may have this activity assessed either as an Extended Individual Contribution or as a Drama-focused activity. A candidate who participates in a formal debate may be assessed, depending on the nature of his or her contribution, for the Individual Extended Contribution or for Group Interaction. (*Guidance on Setting the Centre-Assessed Component: AQA*)

As she put it to me, with the resigned tone of someone who has given up fighting, 'this stuff just kills
the soul'. Yet she is employed because of her soul.
Or, at least, that is how it should be.

Another friend works with both business and
government departments. He tells me that much of
the written material he has to deal with is not only
dismally flat and ugly but also mostly incomprehensible. This sort of thing:

> The structuring team sits within the Equity Deriva-
> tives Group. Its main roles are:
> 1. Product innovation: define and write new pay-
>   offs with sales, traders and quants (pro-active
>   and reactive), participate to the study of the risk
>   management of the new payoffs. The objective
>   is to increase sharply the amount of pro-active
>   business.

This is meaningless drivel. You could try to defend
it by arguing that it is not designed to be understood
by those of us who are not involved in this business,
but that won't do. It is meaningless not only to you
and me: my friend says it is meaningless to him and
most of his colleagues. At any rate, that is the way
they treat it.

But so what? Does a dog look back with regret
to the little pile he has left slap bang in the middle

of the pavement? All that mattered to him was that he produced it, felt relieved, and moved on. Someone else will clean up after him – or possibly not.

I suspect that the person who produces verbal excrement thinks of it in a similar vein. Let someone else worry about it. Words are not there to mean anything. They are there to be processed. They are to be pushed around, shuffled about, entered on the appropriate computer file and then everyone can go home. And if he has no real idea what some of the words really mean – such as 'paradigm' or 'iterate' or 'step change' – there's no problem. Neither does anyone else. But they won't challenge him just in case he really does know and they'd look fools for not knowing. Neat, isn't it?

Speaking and writing, listening and reading should be a pleasure. Meaningless language undermines its whole purpose. If we haven't anything to say, shouldn't we just shut up? Maybe we shall end up grunting at each other.

Yes, I know this is an exaggeration. We all manage to communicate one way or another every day. But the way much language is used suggests we need to ask some pretty fundamental questions.

What Is Language For?

Language distinguishes us from other animals. You may dispute that if you have a teenage son. His grunt when you try to get him out of bed at noon may not seem much different from that of a lowland gorilla, but he will become marginally more articulate when he tells you why he must borrow the car and why you should pay to fill it with petrol. When you say no, the words will flow. A great torrent of them. He will not stop until he has made you understand that you are arguably the worst parent a child ever had and he hates you and intends leaving home immediately – or as soon as his dirty clothes have been washed and ironed.

We need language because we have something else other animals don't seem to have: the imperative to bestow meaning on the world. This is our great glory. On one level it gives us the ability to row with our children rather than just hit them smartly on the side of the head. On the other, all art and literature, science and our material progress flow from this capacity for meaning. It also gets us into a lot of trouble.

Animals may be nasty to each other but it is almost always because they won't survive if they are not. Once the needs of survival are provided for, they tend not to cause too much bother to each other. The lion may indeed lie down with the lamb if his stomach is full. We, on the other hand, go to war with each other not only for reasons of survival but because we clash over the meaning of things.

Still, there is no way round it. Generating meaning is what human beings uniquely do and language is the medium in which we do it.

What Is Good English?

A simple enough question, but it's not easy to answer.

We can all produce our own list of qualities. Mine would include the following: clear, simple, plain and unambiguous. Those are the essentials. It should be free of jargon, although there will be exceptions. It should be easy to read and listen to rather than a chore. At the very least it should not make our tongues fur up. You will add to that list.

But making lists and ticking boxes doesn't really get us anywhere. You cannot judge language in the same way that you test a car when its MOT has expired. It is possible to catch a butterfly, pin it to a board and study its anatomy, but its essence has vanished. To appreciate what an extraordinary creature it is you need to see it in flight, or settling on a buddleia, flapping and closing its fragile wings before it sets off to fly thousands of miles to another continent.

Language is always on the wing. It cannot be examined and analysed to see whether it works, any more than you can study a pinned butterfly and understand how it can navigate those vast distances without compass or computer. Sure, a sentence can be broken down into its component parts. It might pass all the tests set for it by the most rigorous grammarian and still make you want to remove your own liver out of sheer boredom.

Different strokes . . .

Here's another reason why the checklist approach does not work. It is too narrow. It tempts us to equate good English with the sort of English spoken only by the most articulate, educated, self-confident among us: the Jonathan Millers and Stephen Frys of this world. Yes, I know it can be a joy to listen to them, but why do they never have to fumble for a word? Do they have any idea how irritating it is for the rest of humanity when they seem never to struggle to find the right way to end the sentence and can always find the perfect quotation to prove their point? These are the masters of the universe, envied and admired. You will never catch one of them committing the sins of lesser men.

I once interviewed a man who seemed to know quite a lot but who ended almost every answer with 'etc., etc., etc.'. I wanted to snap at him, 'Look, if you have more to say, then damn well say it!' I didn't, of course. You seldom do on these occasions. Another enormous irritation is the fashionable 'whatever'. I suppose it is meant to be cool or trendy – or maybe it's just laziness. And yet there are circumstances when it seems to fit the bill perfectly.

Imagine the teenager slouching off to the job centre and being offered a choice between stacking shelves and gutting chickens. This is the same young man who was told that if he got a few GCSEs the world would be his oyster. So he says to the man behind the desk, 'Yeah . . . whatever.' It expresses how he feels. He has no idea where his life is going and, right now, making decisions is too much trouble. All he wants to do is earn enough to get by and he doesn't much care how he does it. What better way to express all this than the listless 'whatever'? In its own way it is good English.

Language is there to express the entire range of moods and feelings. Uniformity breeds sterility. You would not expect – or want – members of the Long Room at Lord's to speak in the same way as the young braves cheering on Millwall. Nor, God forbid, vice versa.

None of this presents a problem. We will all use more than one language. The words we speak to our bank manager are different from the language we will share with our lover. We need different languages to lead a full life. Some are so private that it would be presumptuous of others to barge in and complain about the way they are being used. But among these many different Englishes there must be a common one in which the business of public life is transacted – and that's the one to keep an eye on so that it does not become devalued. It is our common language that this book is about.

Our Common Language

Concern for our common language is not primarily about rules.

Rather than assess the way we use language only against a set of pre-ordained criteria, we need to ask a different set of questions. Some of them are obvious.

Is the language comprehensible?

Is the message being communicated effectively or not?

What effect is this language having on me?

Does it stimulate me, making me think?

Does it make me want to respond?

Or does it make me switch off and wish I were somewhere else?

And there is another thing to remember. Language is about beauty. One woman wrote to me with a sad comment on the modern prayer book. She compared it with the older Book of Common Prayer. The new one, she said, 'always reminds me of filling in forms'. If that's the case, it is not good English. It may be adequate. It may follow the rules. But the whole point of a prayer book is to inspire and to engage the emotions. If it does not do that it fails.

Language Is Power

Poor language is more than pointless and ugly: it can be dangerous. Journalists are always interested in power. The first sign that it is being abused may be the misuse of language. If a politician, a business leader, a pressure group or the PR spokesman for any number of public organisations is not using straightforward language that most of us can understand, we should smell a rat.

The big worry, if it doesn't sound too grandiose, is how language is being used to shape our world and to shape what we think. That is why this book is about manipulating language as well as mangling it. But we should look at the mangling first.

When I first thought about this book I wrote an article on language for the *Sunday Times*. The response was quite extraordinary – bigger than I have had on any other subject.

They were all worried – for one reason or another – about the way we use English. It is tempting to believe, having read so many letters, that the nation is united on this subject. It is not. Those who don't care and can see nothing wrong with the way we use the language are unlikely to have gone to the trouble of writing. But they exist, and their attitudes cannot be ignored.

CHAPTER TWO

Who Cares?

Dinosaurs play a large part in the life of my youngest child. We were talking about how many of his vast collection he should take with him to nursery one morning. 'I'm going to take only one,' he announced firmly. And then he repeated it: 'Only one.' He was probably a bit surprised by my reaction.

I swept him up into my arms, hugged and kissed him and wanted to rush out into the street shouting, 'My little boy put "only" in the right place and he's not even four years old yet!' I didn't, thank God, but I did tell people about it in the office the next morning. Big mistake. I could see it in their eyes. Poor little soul, they were thinking, what chance does he have of growing up into a normal human being with a father like that?

Because it dominates your own life you assume colleagues and friends will show at least a passing interest in the book you are writing. Instead they grow visibly uneasy. They murmur, 'How very interesting,' as you begin yet another rant about kids today not being able to write a simple sentence to save their lives. You know what they're thinking: 'Another bloody anorak! God save us from them.' This is hurtful – but possibly true. Better to be an anorak, though, than some other things.

The Slobs

These are people who genuinely do not care about the way language is used. In truth, they don't care about anything very much. Why bother voting? It only encourages the politicians; if it really changed anything it wouldn't be allowed. What if all our libraries are being turned into glitzy video shops? It's what the kids want; keeps 'em off the streets, eh? What if everyone eats 'fast food' these days? Fills you up, dunnit? Just fuel, innit? What's on the telly?

The Yobs

These are worse than the slobs. They pretend not to care about language, but they do. They actually choose to speak it badly. They are a late twentieth-century phenomenon. Many of them were brought up to use perfectly good English but decided some-where along the road to develop what they would probably call 'street cred'. Out went their carefully knotted ties and in came their Estuary English and 'y'knows' and 'like'.

To the extent that it is possible to pinpoint this, it probably began with society gels. It's a while since they called themselves that. Now they are It-girls or posh totty, whichever you prefer. Tara Palmer-Tomkinson is said to have been the first modern It-girl. I asked her once what it means and she said she had no idea.

The yobs once despised the language of Essex Girl, then decided to ape it. Recently, some politicians have joined in. People who study these things notice how Tony Blair's language and delivery change when he is addressing certain audiences.

The Nobs

These are the people who hanker for the days when your station in life was defined by how you spoke: posh people spoke posh English. They try to speak like the Queen or even Brian Sewell, the only man I have ever met who makes the Queen sound common. Those who do not are, by definition, inferior. The nobs hanker for the fifties and the decades before it – the era of deference and forelock-touching. They are a dying breed.

To complicate matters, there are sub-divisions in

this category. There are those who are not very bright and think that 'talking posh' makes them sound brighter. And there are those who are very bright indeed and calculate that talking posh will help their careers. Roy Jenkins (later Lord Jenkins) was in that category.

He was one of the greatest politicians of his generation. He was also God's gift to satire with his famous love of a decent claret, his inability to pronounce his R's and his cut-glass accent that made him sound as though he had been born the son of a duke and had spent his childhood in the grandest drawing rooms of the land. When he wasn't being groomed at Eton he was out on the moors with Pater bagging a few brace of grouse.

In truth he was born the son of a Welsh miner in a terraced house near Abersychan. His father, who became an MP, was jailed in the General Strike of 1926. If the Jenkins family were anything like their neighbours in the Welsh valleys of those years, the closest he'd have come to a decent claret was the sweet sherry kept in the sideboard for Christmas and funerals. But you'd never have guessed it if you'd met him after he'd left the valleys and gone to Oxford.

It is said that Aneurin Bevan was listening to the young Roy's maiden speech in the House of Commons with another MP who observed, 'Smart boy that Jenkins, but they say he's a bit lazy.' Bevan replied, with his famous stammer, 'No b-b-b-boy who comes from Abersychan and c-c-can speak with an accent like that can p-p-possibly be called lazy.'

The Snobs

These are the people who don't want to talk posh but who do want to sound clever. They confuse good English with pretentious English. They like long words even when there is a perfectly good short one. You hear it often, I'm ashamed to say, on the BBC. They always 'attempt' something and never 'try'. They 'enquire' or 'request' and never 'ask'. They are 'prevented from' doing something and never 'stopped'. 'Further' is used instead of 'more' – or, rather, it is 'utilised'. Missing children are never deemed to be back with their parents but always 're-united' with them. And then there is 'elect'. This is deeply irritating. I blame cricket for this one: the captain 'elects' to bat, we are told. No, he doesn't; he chooses.

The Pedants

These are the people who can't pick up a copy of *The Times* without wanting to write about some solecism they spotted on page 17. They think there is only one thing that matters: observing the rules. Every transgression is an outrage. They will avoid a split infinitive however convoluted the resulting sentence may sound. They will cling to the rules until their fingertips bleed and believe any other approach will lead to anarchy. They cannot see a dangling participle without wanting to hang it in the right place. Solecisms are scars on their backs. Poor syntax is the equivalent of a nail scratching on a blackboard. They feel almost physical pain when they see apostrophes in the wrong place and commas where no pause is intended. Reading prose disfigured by bad grammar is a form of torture for them.

The Doubters

Finally there are those who really believe in good English but are a bit unsure of themselves. They care for the language and how it sounds, but find rules a bit offputting. They sometimes feel a little out of their depth. Although they don't much like to admit it openly, they are not too sure exactly what the rules are.

Nature or Nurture?

The category you fall into may depend on the teacher you had at school. If you are of a certain era you would have had Miss Smythe, who wore sensible tweed skirts and who made you stand up when she came into the classroom and chant, 'Good morning, Miss Smythe'. If you were of another era you might have had Ms Smith, who wore short skirts and crop tops if the Head let her get away with it and rather enjoyed talking about her boyfriends to the children.

Miss Smythe did not have a boyfriend and if she had she would not have talked about him – most certainly not to children who had no business knowing about such things. She stood sternly at the front of the class, all seated in neat rows at wooden desks that smelt of polish, and drilled grammar into her charges. You spoke only to chant back at her the rules she wrote on the blackboard. The rules were God-given. There was no argument or discussion. You cannot argue with God – or Miss Smythe. You were not required to show enthusiasm – just attention. She taught. You listened. If you were in her class you might well have turned out to be a pedant, but you will certainly be able to write a letter to your bank manager – and to *The Times*.

Ms Smith's class sat in little plastic chairs around

communal tables. They chatted among themselves. Ms Smith was trained to believe that 'kids' could not be taught if they were not interested. Everything centred on the children. The trick was to arouse their enthusiasm. Rigid rules tended to get in the way of that. Children will learn what they need to learn only if they can be inspired. Order was not important. Babel was better than boredom.

Yet Ms Smith cared about English too. She wanted her young charges to be creative with words and excited by what they could do with them. If you were in her class you may still be excited by words. That excitement has never gone. It is why I care about how language is used but don't get too upset when the odd rule is broken.

There is a hint of caricature in this, I grant you. But the clash between the two approaches is at the heart of the argument over good English. If you do not already recognise the tension between the two, then I suggest you go out and acquire a very small child.

Out of the Mouths ...

Listening to a child learning to speak is one of the most exciting, rewarding, frustrating, exhilarating experiences life has to offer. Part of the joy comes from the total candour of small children. They may be cunning in many different ways – they always seem to know which parent will give in first – but not with language. It takes a while to learn the art of euphemism. If a small child thinks you are thin or fat or ugly he will say so – and want to know why.

But it is also a mysterious process. Why is it that one child will be gabbling away almost before he can sit up straight and another refuses to utter more than an indistinct 'Mama' until his parents begin to give up hope? Or, if they are middle class, have to remortgage the house to pay for the therapists and child psychiatrists' fees. Then, one day and for absolutely no discernible reason, he speaks. The sentences come out perfectly formed and it's obvious that he has been working it out in his head all this time. He was probably looking at his parents all along and thinking, 'Why do they make such a fuss? I'll speak when I'm ready.'

For a child, the only rule is that there are no rules. If children can't find the right words they make them up. That is an education in itself. So a police car becomes a 'wah-wah' because that's the noise it makes, and a football player becomes a 'scorer man' because that's what he does. If 'yesterday' or last night' is a difficult notion for a three-year-old to grasp, it becomes (as with my little boy) 'last earlier'. It works perfectly. If the past tense is proving troublesome, they just add 'ed' and you get 'slided' instead of 'slid' or 'standed' instead of 'stood'.

Children who have learned just enough words and structure to form basic sentences are a particular joy to listen to. That is partly because they have no concept of patience. It is alien to them. Instead they have enthusiasm. They do not take their time, trying carefully to explain what they want to say. Instead they rush at the sentences like a character in a Disney cartoon being chased by a monster, their words all jumbling together until they run out of breath and gasp for air before they rush on to the next thought. Sometimes it works; sometimes it doesn't. Usually you get a sense of what they are trying to say.

Eventually they begin correcting themselves. They respond to the way we speak. But some errors persist and we correct them because we know they will be at a disadvantage if we do not. The point linguistic theorists make is that the *capacity* to use language is innate, deep-wired. It is the same in all of us and pretty much immune to change or interference. But the *practice* of language is conventional. It depends wholly on the conventions adopted by the society and culture into which we happen to have been born.

When to Worry

This can cause problems. I enjoyed the following exchange between a French woman and her English friend, each with a one-year-old. Only the names have been changed to protect from embarrassment.

'We're a little bit bothered about Antoine. He hasn't said anything yet, and we think perhaps he ought to have done so by now. Has Anthony?'

'No, not really. He seems to be on the verge of it but it's a bit difficult to tell. Though we did think last week he may have said "duck".'

A look of competitive horror crossed Antoine's mother's face. Then she marshalled her forces. 'Well, of course,' she said, 'in French "duck" is "*canard*" and that would be far too difficult for a child of Antoine's age to say!'

The trick at this stage, I suspect, is never to make comparisons. Well, almost never. You should probably start getting a bit worried if your son is still calling a police car a wah-wah when its driver picks him up drunk from the gutter at the age of seventeen. But there are relatively few youngsters who do not eventually master the art of speaking in one form or another. Even if they never quite get the hang of communicating properly it may not be a complete disaster. They simply become professional football players, earn £50,000 a week and employ a publicity agent to speak on their behalf. Or they become politicians and their spin doctors teach them a set of formulas, which they trot out whenever the occasion demands it.

Good English should have all the vitality, inventiveness and sheer enthusiasm of a small child learning how wonderful it is to be able to make himself understood. It respects some discipline. Discipline does not limit: it liberates. It is what makes it possible to do the job – the job of communicating. This is how Alexander Pope put it three centuries ago.

True ease in writing comes from art, not chance
As those move easiest who have learned to dance.

The question is, how much discipline do we need?

CHAPTER THREE

The Need To Be Taught

It was 4.30 a.m. and I was bashing away at my keyboard. I was in my usually sunny mood for that time in the morning: smiling graciously to all and sundry; a cheerful quip about the fact that the taxi had been late and I had been kept waiting in bitter cold outside my house; warm praise for the delightful producer who had put together a programme running order that pleased me in every respect. You don't believe me? Fair enough. I was in a foul mood and looking for a reason to have a row with someone.

It arrived on my screen a few minutes later. The way it works on *Today* is that producers and reporters suggest to the presenters links (or 'cues', in our jargon) for the different items. We then rewrite them, honing them to perfection – or, if you prefer to take the producers' word for it, ripping the heart out of them and turning them into a parody of what was intended. The one on my screen was a monster. There was every cliché in the book and then some.

It was illiterate, verging on the grotesque. I exploded.

'Who wrote this pile of sh . . . t!' I assumed it had been written by one of the producers on the previous 'day shift'. Instead, a quiet voice behind me said, 'I did.' Oh, God. It's one thing, in the time-honoured way of lily-livered journalists the world over, to tear someone apart when they're not there to defend themselves. It is quite another to do it when the poor chap is sitting three feet away. I braced myself for either a grovelling apology or a cup of coffee poured on my head. Instead, he pointed at a story on the front page of the *Independent*. It was about me making an attack on bad English. His cue had been a hoax and I had fallen for it. The slightly scary thing was that I had believed it was genuine.

It would be ungracious of me – and, indeed, unfair – to attack my colleagues on *Today*. They are a clever, enthusiastic, hard-working and talented young bunch and it's a pleasure to work with them. They are also well educated and have the degrees to prove it. What few have is any grounding in grammar. To many of them punctuation and syntax are enduring mysteries. They are not remarkable in this. It is true of almost all the young people I have worked with for many years. They simply weren't taught these disciplines at school. And that's because it was deemed that they needed protecting from people engaged in a terrible conspiracy.

The Conspiracy Theorists

Conspiracy theorists are always good fun. You didn't know that JFK was killed by an evil alliance between alien lizards and Elvis Presley? Where have you been? Then there's all that rubbish about man going to the moon. Only the truly naïve believe that one. The so-called 'moon landing' was staged in a big barn in Arizona to get the President re-elected, wasn't it? And of course Harold Wilson was a Communist spy and Margaret Thatcher was really a man.

It was back in the sixties that liberal educationists discovered their conspiracy. It ran something like this. The teaching of English was being controlled by the ruling class and we, the lumpen proletariat, were victims of class oppression. We were being told how to speak and write and, downtrodden as we were, we conformed. We were encouraged to give up our natural and authentic manner of speaking and we didn't even know what was happening to us because, as one of the funniest television sketches of all time told us, we 'knew our place'.

All this was part of a much wider war in which the enemy was not just the British upper classes with their Home Counties English, it was Great

Literature. Who, after all, had set the standards for good English to which we should all aspire? The great writers of the past. And who were they? Why, they were Dead White Males (and Jane Austen and George Eliot, of course). Why should we touch our forelocks to them when they themselves were mostly toffs of a different era perpetuating the prejudices and injustices of their time? Thank God the liberals spotted it and came to our rescue!

This conspiracy theory was always daft. If the liberals had stopped to think for a moment they would have realised that the way to win a battle with your oppressor is to use his own weapons against him. In this case, the weapon of good English. The daft theory became so widely accepted that it effectively destroyed the teaching of good English.

Mark My Words

The effect was catastrophic and has been described in countless letters I have received over the years. A French woman wrote:

> I worked for thirty years as a translator (French to English) for a French oil company. When I contracted work out, for a long time I was puzzled by the very poor standard of the

translations by translators who claimed that their mother tongue was English. It took me a while to cotton on to the fact that they may have had a good knowledge of French but they did not know how to write their own language correctly.

A man in his sixties went back to school to learn German in a class of younger adults. He became used to 'the teacher crying in exasperation to the class: "How can I teach you the language when you do not understand grammar!"' Another man who had been teaching English as a foreign language for more than thirty years now finds that he has to teach his students two English languages: 'The irony is that foreigners who learn English abroad can understand each other while the only English speakers they cannot understand are now the English themselves.' And an Indian woman with a Cambridge degree ruefully remarked: 'Asking a randomly picked speaker of this easy, wonderfully expressive language about the accusative case is hardly likely to get me more than accusatory stares about the state of my mental balance.'

An exaggeration? Well, maybe, but many academics don't seem to think so. A professor at one of our leading universities told me he had seen literacy among undergraduates 'declining alarmingly over the past decade'.

Ten years ago Sir Michael Dummett, who had just retired as a professor of logic at Oxford, felt the need to write a little book, *Grammar and Style*, simply to instruct students taking exams on how to answer the questions. This was not about the content of their answers, just how to write them. They were supposed to be among the brightest young people in the country and yet they were unable to do what was once expected of children who had just finished primary school.

A survey of university vice chancellors in the summer of 2004 revealed that 48 per cent had had to introduce special lessons in literacy and numeracy for first-year students. Their efforts are not always appreciated.

You Fascist!

One of the things professors often do when they mark examination scripts is scribble in the margins. I know of one professor who was in the habit of deducting marks for bad spelling, poor grammar or clumsy sentences that failed to express the ideas clearly. He would scribble in the margins to tell the candidate what he had done and why. He no longer does that. He is afraid that if his marking is challenged and an appeal conducted, he will be held to have been discriminatory. This is not only silly on an heroic scale, it is deeply depressing.

Another said that when he had underlined some spelling errors in a student's essay the student replied: 'What are you? Some sort of spelling fascist?' In my dreams I imagine the student on an operating-table. Just as the anaesthetist is about to knock him out he notices that the surgeon's breath reeks of whisky and the hand holding the scalpel shakes violently. When he objects the surgeon says: 'What are you? Some sort of teetotal fascist?'

If you want to play football for Arsenal you need to be able to kick a ball. If you want to aspire to any sort of academic achievement you need to be able to express yourself clearly. How can you assess the quality of someone's mind if they can't tell you what they know and how they think? This has nothing to do with class wars and the oppression of the workers by their well-spoken superiors. It has nothing to do with who controls the language and why. We all do. Or, at least, we all should.

Lets Do It

Most alarming is that many teachers themselves seem not to have learned the basics of the language they will end up teaching. One woman wrote to tell me:

When I left teacher training college in 1983, despite my academic qualifications, I had no idea what the difference between a noun and a verb was. I still struggle with the split infinitive, word order and the other essential parts of grammar in the language I love and speak.

But perhaps we're getting to the stage where it's not thought important for either teachers or pupils to know about this sort of thing. In the summer of 2004 a GCSE examiner wrote to Alice Miles of *The Times* to complain about the way he was required to mark scripts. He wrote:

> I was also forced to award ludicrously high marks to candidates whose command of English grammar and/or sentence structure was simply non-existent. Upwards of 150 candidates will have been awarded a C (or better) who wrote 'could of', 'might of', 'should of'. The pronouns I and me were used interchangeably by large numbers of candidates (as in 'Me and Mr Birling have done nothing wrong' or 'The Inspector was so rude to Mr Birling and I'). *Neighbours*-speak was quite common, as in 'Then Shelia [*sic*] was like, what?' (meaning she was surprised, I supposed).

And some distinguished academics seem to give succour to it.

Here is Jean Aitchison, Reith lecturer and formerly the Rupert Murdoch Professor of Language and Communication at Oxford. In her book, *Language Change: Progress or Decay*, she takes a very relaxed view about whether or not we need bother with the apostrophe in the word 'let's'. She offers us some scholarly explanation of what linguists call, not without some difficulty, 'grammaticalisation'. It means the process by which phrases in common use get pruned down. A good example is the Latin '*mea domina*' (my lady) being reduced via French '*ma dame*' to 'ma'am' and even to 'm'. All very interesting. But then she writes this:

> *Let's*, perhaps now better spelled *lets*, is used as a simple exhortation, and is no longer thought of as a verb plus a pronoun.

Can this be true? A respected academic condoning such vandalism? She may be right about it no longer being thought of as a verb plus a pronoun. I doubt that it ever was – not by most of us anyway. We just knew the basic rule – it was there because it was shorthand for 'let us' – and that was all we wanted or needed to know. Now we are told not to worry about any of it: lets just forget the rule. No. Most linguists are adamant that they should only describe how languages work rather than lay down the law – yet they are happy to come up with their own recommendations when the mood takes them. I wonder where this sort of revisionism ends. No doubt we shall eventually have academics telling us it's okay to say, 'I could of danced all night,' on the basis that 'of' has become an acceptable 'grammaticalisation' of 'have'.

Far from liberating or helping the young, this sort of nonsense is more likely to harm them. As this former teacher put it:

> It is easy to choose to dumb down when you are suitably equipped with all the skills and tools you need to navigate your way around the language. What tends to be forgotten is that those who are 'dumbed down' to, have no choice but to take the educational menu that is offered them. Those encouraged to take this inferior educational diet will never hope to achieve the literacy skills that their 'dumbing down' masters already possess. To sum up, a student once said to me: 'I want to know what you know.'

Safe Software

There is a radical view that says we need not bother with any of this because it will all be taken care of anyway. We have technology to save us now. We need merely click on an icon and our computer will not only correct our spelling but deal with our faulty grammar too. Like hell it will. Spelling is something it can just about handle, so long as we watch it very carefully indeed and do not allow it to turn our English into American. But I would prefer to allow that drunken surgeon to operate on my brain with a chainsaw than allow a computer to correct my grammar.

I suppose you can't really call it stupid because it is, after all, only a machine. But you *can* call the people who wrote the software stupid . . . and ignorant . . . and bloody impertinent as well. Writing is a subtle business. The rule that works perfectly well for one sentence will not work for another. It's the same with punctuation. I have a horror of people who invariably put a comma before 'and'. The whole point of 'and' is that it replaces the comma. But not always. It is correct to write: 'He went to Oxford and he also went to London.' It is also correct to write: 'He went to Oxford and, because he had time to spare, he also went to London.'

Can a computer cope with that pretty basic

difference? Can it recognise a parenthesis when it sees one? No, it cannot. Even if it spots a howler you cannot trust it to correct it intelligently. We would not rely on a computer to write decent prose so let's not pretend it can manage the infinitely more limited task of writing decent grammar either. Even if the damn thing got it right I would be against it.

We cannot control language if we do not understand how it works. I've no idea what happens under the bonnet of a modern car with all its computers and wizardry, but it doesn't matter: so long as the engine works the car moves. It's not like that with language.

CHAPTER FOUR

Usage Rules

I doubt there are many people who actually want to read bad grammar, but there are an awful lot of people who despise pedants. My friend and former editor, Rod Liddle, is to pedantry what a dog is to a lamp-post. He cannot see a rule without wanting to cock his leg against it. He was fired from the BBC for writing rude things about the government (editors of the *Today* programme are not meant to do that) and is a born iconoclast. He is also one of the most promising writers of his generation. Maybe there's a connection somewhere; show him a sacred cow and he will slaughter it on the spot. So when Lynne Truss wrote her admirable book on punctuation, *Eats, Shoots & Leaves*, Rod naturally wrote a column for *The Times* attacking it.

It was, as you would expect from Rod, clever and funny. It was also virtually unreadable because, apart from full stops, he used no punctuation. His point was that we would understand what he was saying perfectly well. Indeed we did. But it wasn't half hard work.

Take one of the sentences in my last paragraph and remove the commas: 'It was as you would expect clever and funny.' Its meaning is clear once you have paused for a second to work it out. But the great strength of commas in the right place is that you don't have to pause and think. They do the job for you. That's why they are there. They remove ambiguity and make the task of reading so much easier. Correct punctuation enables you to devote your full attention to what is written rather than the way the sentence is constructed. But I don't want to trespass on Truss territory. Her book sold like iced water in a heatwave because it was well written and everyone who read it could follow her argument – including, of course, Rod.

The Polystyrene Moment

Why do so many despise pedants? Probably because they are often people who know more than we do and are not afraid to say so. They can't win. If people know less than we do we call them ignorant; if they know more we call them pedants. Nor is it true that they are all in their twilight years with nothing better to do than search out nits to pick.

Here's part of a letter I received following my *Sunday Times* article:

> A preposition should never, ever end a sentence.
> Ever. On pain of death. OK, maybe not on pain
> of death, but at least on pain of angry stares and
> a good deal of sulking . . . To me it's the verbal
> equivalent of two bits of polystyrene rubbing
> together: unbearable.

The letter was written by a seventeen-year-old A-level student. What was wonderful about it was her strength of feeling. As it happens, I agree with her about polystyrene but not about prepositions. Mostly it is better not to end sentences with one, but not always.

Let's worry about the really big things. If the pedants of the world are to unite, they need to decide the territory they want to fight on or (to spare my correspondent's agony) the territory on which they want to fight. Some things matter a great deal; most do not. Some rules even beg to be broken occasionally. 'Boldly to go' sounds pretty limp compared with the original. But mostly there is no reason to split an infinitive, and if it causes grief to others, why do it?

We all have our polystyrene moments. Another of mine is 'than twice as much than'. I mention it

because I saw it in *The Times* a few moments ago.
I understood the sentence perfectly well, of course,
but it was irritating. And I hate seeing 'almost
unique' or 'nearly unprecedented'. Again, you get
the drift, but that's not good enough. Unique is . . .
well . . . unique. If it is qualified it loses its whole
point and that's a pity.

Dancing and Boozing . . .

It is the sloppy and the downright pernicious that
must be attacked. I suppose most of us can agree
with that GCSE examiner on the worst excesses: 'I
could of danced all night.' How can anyone do it?
How can anyone write the preposition 'of' instead
of the verb 'have'? It makes no sense at all and yet
it is creeping in. It is just about possible to see why.
In spoken English 'of' sounds a bit like 'have' and
there are, sadly, many people out there who do not
distinguish between the two. But it is a big leap
from the spoken to the written. Even the trendiest,
most laid-back young teacher should blanch at that
one – or so you would think. Now read this:

I'm sure you could of written it alot neater.

Three howlers in one sentence. I would like to tell
you I invented it to make a point, or that it was

written by a drunken Latvian whose English lessons finished thirty years ago. Neither, I'm afraid. It was written at the bottom of an eight-year-old's essay by her primary-school teacher. God help the eight-year-old. God help every child in her class.

The teacher may be brilliant in many ways. Her young charges may end up with a high degree of self-awareness and oodles of enthusiasm for every subject under the sun. They may be imaginative, creative and thoughtful. What they will not be able to do is write simple English. Even if they turn out to be the leading figures in their chosen fields they will have difficulty in expressing their thoughts.

Those were easy illustrations. This one is more likely to divide opinion even among those who claim to care about English:

> If I'd have been out boozing half the night, I'd have been pretty useless presenting the *Today* programme the following morning.

No confusion between 'of' and 'have' there, so what's the problem? Certainly the truth of the sentiment is undeniable. I tried it once – admittedly in the very early days of my *Today* career. I was so badly hung-over when I staggered in to work that I could barely function. Half-way through a live interview with a distinguished politician I realised that I had not only lost the thread of the argument but I couldn't remember his name. I never did it again. But it is the grammar we are concerned with. This is what I should have written:

> If I'd been out boozing all night I'd have been pretty useless . . .

Perhaps you read the original sentence without batting an eyelid. It is the sort of language we use in everyday conversation. You will know what I was trying to say. But you may be banging the table in fury because it breaks rules that matter to you. The extra 'have' is redundant and one criterion for good English is its economy. It also happens to be ugly, though I accept that beauty is in the eye of the beholder.

. . . or Just a Nice Cup of Tea

The genial Mr Brooke in George Eliot's *Middlemarch* offered some good advice that should probably be taken on board by extreme pedants. His unvarying refrain, especially when he was faced with a new enthusiasm on the part of his daughter Dorothea, was something along these lines: 'Well, my dear, I went into that sort of thing, too, when I was young. But you can take these things too far, you know.'

Indeed you can. Extreme pedantry is a sort of virus that gets into the blood, so that its victims start seeing ambiguity where none exists. They see this sign:

Dogs must be carried on escalator.

They know perfectly well that no one is about to dash off to the nearest pet shop and buy a dog before they will be allowed to use the escalator, but they still get agitated. Just as they might worry about the sign I saw outside a hospital:

Thieves operate in this car park.

Yes, yes, we all know the NHS has problems but honestly . . .

You may think I'm joking but you'd be surprised by the number of letters I have had from people who get genuinely cross about this sort of thing. They see a sign that says 'disabled toilet' and they want it fixed. 'Alarmed doors' is another: what happened to scare them? Nor do they like 'a solo concert' or 'serious fun' or even 'a nice cup of tea'. You have to be off the scale of extreme pedantry even to contemplate the notion that it's the cup that is nice. But contemplate it they will. A cup of nice tea is what they want.

One answer is to accept 'cuppa' into the *Oxford English Dictionary* and have done with it. It's rather a good word. It is wholly unambiguous. It could not possibly mean a cup of coffee, though I have no idea why not, and it would serve its purpose very well. I hereby submit it to dictionary compilers.

The pedantry virus is highly infectious and I am not immune. I had a delightful letter from someone who made one or two good points about grammatical failings. She ended by describing herself as a 'retired woman'. I spent a few happy minutes trying to imagine why she felt the need to retire from being a woman – and what she had become instead.

Irritable Vowel Syndrome

People do get very cross about perceived solecisms:

> I reserve my greatest irritation for people who use
> the words 'whose' or 'who' for non-human
> subjects and the use of plural verbs for singular or
> collective nouns.

Well, that correspondent was undoubtedly right. Sloppy language is to be deplored. But 'greatest irritation'?

Sometimes there is the whiff of hidden agendas:

Is this perpetual abuse of our language due to egali-
tarianism, the influence of our transatlantic allies
or some other cause?

That's the stuff! Can't be doing with all this egali-
tarianism nonsense myself. Things have been going
downhill ever since bleeding-heart liberals started
encouraging snotty-nosed working-class urchins to
read. Gave 'em ideas above their station. Country's
been going to the dogs ever since.

I'd love to know what my choleric correspondent's 'other cause' might be. Getting rid of the
birch, perhaps. I did, though, feel a twinge of pity
for another correspondent, who appreciates the distinction in English between the comparative and the
superlative:

It is such a pity that Anne Robinson does not
exploit it when she has two contestants left but
still calls one of them the 'weakest link' (not
'weaker'). Similarly, in the final round it should be
'whoever answers more questions correctly', but
she insists on saying 'the most'. I have written to
her about this but she ignores my letter and has
not sent me the signed photo I asked for.

47

What can one say? The man is right. Of course he is right. Yet somehow one is not too surprised that he has never received his signed photograph.

I think this woman has a sound case:

> I hate to be a nit-picking old bag, but when you had grammar lessons at school you were taught it was so important.

It is important, but she's right to worry about the effect of pedantry on people who have other, more important, things to worry about. The trick is to do a bit less nit-picking and point-scoring and worry about those things. Grammatical errors do not prove moral degeneracy any more than perfect syntax is evidence of a soul bound for heaven. Rules, valuable though some may be, are never enough and there are good reasons for that.

Some of the rules are bogus. Many are quite recent, invented in the eighteenth and nineteenth centuries by grammarians who thought that if English were to be a properly respectable language it was about time it had some. Hence the publication of Bishop Lowth's *Short Introduction to English Grammar* in 1762. Much of what we ended up with was an adaptation for English of Latin grammar. But English is only partly a Latinate language. My Latin education ended when I was thirteen, which is a pity. It puts you at a serious disadvantage against people who went to posh schools and can trot out elegant Latin phrases as if they really understand what they mean. All I can remember is that Latin phrases were so precise that it didn't much matter what order the words were in: the sentence still made sense.

The split infinitive is a fine example of a bogus rule. You cannot split infinitives in Latin because they are single words. But the classicists decided we needed to have a rule, so we have one: it is wrong to split the infinitive. That seems to be the extent of the logic. One of my correspondents made a good point: 'English is English, not a debased form of Latin.'

Language Changes

There's another reason why blind devotion to rules won't do. Language must change. Even the most extreme pedant should acknowledge that. If it did not change it would stay the same. How's that for stating the obvious? Yet many hanker for the language of Shakespeare or Milton or Dickens. How rich their language sounds as we read and hear it today. What a great deal we have lost. Well, up to a point. If we spoke in the language of Shakespeare today there would be no way of describing It-girls or soap operas or Premier League football. So it wouldn't necessarily be all bad. But on balance the drawbacks would outweigh the benefits.

The question is not whether language should change but how. This is why it is a mistake to talk about 'defending' the language. Defence implies building barricades or digging ditches. It is about keeping the invader out, rather than allowing him in and winning him over to your side. Instead of defending every lost cause that comes limping down the pike we should be finding ways to keep what is vital and exploiting the infinite capacity of language to grow and enrich itself. Language serves us well when it allows us to be become ever more expressive.

There are dozens of different forces acting on language at any one time and some have the power to do the opposite of that. Instead of encouraging ever greater subtlety and refinement they coarsen and diminish. Taken to the most absurd extreme, Hamlet's soliloquy would (as various wags have pointed out) go something like this: 'To be or not to be . . . whatever.'

So, the point here is simple. If something expands our power of expression it is good, but if it limits it, it is bad. It is very bad indeed when words with clearly different meanings are used interchangeably. Distinction expands our scope for expression. Its removal constrains it.

Who's Interested?

Alastair Campbell and I had a number of professional disagreements during his last few years in
10 Downing Street – by which I mean he kept trying
to get me sacked from one job or another. On one
occasion he had a henchman write to my boss at
the BBC demanding that 'something be done about
the John Humphrys problem'. My offence, so far
as I could tell, was to show insufficient respect to
cabinet ministers. We had different views as to how
a political interviewer should go about his job. He
once wrote to the *Guardian* to point out that I was
not the Queen Mother. Pity all his observations
weren't as accurate.

At the end of one interview with Tony Blair, who
was 'down the line' from his home in his constitu-
ency, Alastair ripped off the headphones, leaned
across the table and uttered just one word:
'Wanker!' My producer, who was there at the time
and told me about it, said he wasn't absolutely sure
to whom Alastair was referring. But I had to wait
for years before being granted another interview
with the Prime Minister. Such is life.

When Campbell left Downing Street he turned to
different ways of earning a crust. One was offering
advice to people who needed to smarten up their
communication strategy. You and I would think of

it as a spin doctor's master class. One such course was called (so the *Mail on Sunday* reported): 'How to Handle a Cynical and Disinterested Media'.

The possibility that Alastair regards the media as disinterested – meaning dispassionate, without any axe to grind – is about as great as Tony Blair being the secret love child of John Prescott and Margaret Thatcher. Even though Campbell worked as a journalist for many years – possibly because of it – he takes the view that most of us are pretty low down the evolutionary scale.

No, he got it wrong. The sad truth is that he or his representative simply did not know the difference between that and 'uninterested'.

It is a terrible thing to kill a good word. Once the word is lost, it is lost for ever. It has happened to 'repel'. Read this sentence from one of the *Independent*'s brightest young columnists, Johann Hari:

> I'm not sentimental about animals, and the people who obsess about the rights of animals while neglecting those of humans repulse me.

Put aside the use of 'obsess' as a verb; it's ugly but at least it is functional and there can be no mistaking its meaning. But 'repulse' when he meant 'repel'? He might very well be repulsed if he launched a physical attack on those obsessive people, but I don't think that's what he meant.

Lost Tempers

When Humpty Dumpty told Alice in *Through the Looking Glass* that words meant just what he chose them to mean, neither more nor less, she was not convinced. 'The question is,' she said, 'whether you *can* make words mean different things.'

The answer, my dear Alice, is that you can. We do it all the time and it is, at best, unsettling. God help the foreigner who has to deal with the way words end up meaning the opposite of what was originally intended. Try this sentence:

'I had a terrible temper and I lost it.'

A foreigner who knew no more than the simple meaning of English words might take from this that I once had a terrible temper but now I had lost it and so had become a calm, equable soul, endlessly patient with call centres, badly behaved children and dissimulating politicians. But, of course, it does not mean that. The word 'temper' has gone through 180 degrees.

It once meant 'good temper' – moderate, controlled, relaxed – and that meaning persists in some versions of the word. We 'temper our criticism' and we have a 'fine temperament'. Then it came to mean the opposite. Temper meant anger. And now losing your temper – in the new sense of the word – para-doxically means keeping it. If I told you I was in a fine old temper you would be in no doubt what I meant.

English is full of this sort of idiomatic somersault. The word 'presently' once meant 'now' (at present), but has come to mean 'soon'. 'Candour' is an inter-esting one. It comes from the same Latin root that produces 'candescence' and meant 'brilliant white-ness'. Then, three hundred years ago, it was used to describe speech and meant 'purity, innocence'. That too developed so that candour in speech came to mean lacking false additions, such as those that diplomacy or even courtesy might insert. Candid speaking then became blunt speaking. Politicians still use it a lot these days. Alastair Campbell often said he was speaking 'candidly'. Alastair the Inno-cent? I don't think so.

Candid Camera

Mostly these things matter only to academic types, but they can cause trouble in the wrong hands. A certain Geoffrey Oakshott wrote to me about his difficulties with 'candid'. He is a photographer. 'In order,' as he put it, 'to avoid being asked to do formal groups and weddings ... I put "informal and candid photography" on my business cards.' The result was the following exchange of emails:

Hello Mr Oakshott. My wife and I have seen some of your photographs and note that you take candid and informal photographs. Without wishing to be offensive, we wondered whether 'candid' included photographs of couples. We are seeking a professional photographer to take candid photographs of us (nothing extreme). Would you be able to accept such a commission? Would you prefer to photograph us in your studio or in our home?

He replied:

Dear Sir
I think we may have different interpretations of the word 'candid'. I use it in the same sense as Candid Camera, i.e. unrehearsed, unposed, engaged in those normal activities of daily life which may be seen at any time in public places by people of all ages.

Apologies if I have misinterpreted the tone of your email.

And he got this back:

Dear Mr Oakshott
Many thanks for your message. I am not sure that the candid photographs my wife and I had in mind would be suitable for viewing in public places. We will seek another candidate.

Innit?

Usage and construction change almost as much as vocabulary. Imagine it is breakfast time (incidentally, I wonder why so few of us 'take' breakfast these days) and there is the usual mayhem: small child refusing to eat because you have run out of those cereals that would make a scavenging fox vomit; middle child complaining because her favourite top hasn't been ironed; oldest still in bed because that's what teenagers do in the mornings. You look at your watch. 'Damn!' you call to your wife. 'I'm going to be late for the train, aren't I?'

Now where did that come from: 'aren't I'? You don't go around saying, 'I are,' so why should it be 'Aren't I?' If rules mean anything, surely that should be ruled out straight away. But I doubt that you are too bothered about it one way or the other. Neither am I. Yet some people would rather be seen naked in public than be heard saying, 'Aren't I?' Instead they say, 'Am I not?' That's all very well, but it has a distinct whiff of m'learned friends about it:

'I am right in thinking the murder weapon was covered with your fingerprints, am I not?'

Yet it doesn't seem quite right over the breakfast table.

'Damn! I'm going to be late for the train, am I not?'

Try it at home and your children will probably tell you to get a life.

So here's another variation on the theme:

'Damn! I'm going to be late for the train, innit?'

In theory your children should approve. That's what Ali G would say. They probably say it all the time. It has become cool. It has street cred. In practice they will regard you with the contempt they reserve for middle-aged fathers on the dance-floor trying to do anything more modern than a foxtrot. You would be deemed to be making a fool of yourself, than which there is no greater offence in the eyes of the young. Yet why should 'innit' be the preserve of teenagers? The French do it all the time with '*n'est ce pas*', which is a direct translation.

Here is my final thought on the subject.

'Damn! I'm going to be late for the train, ain't I?'

The drawback is that you will sound like one of the accused in a Dickens novel:

'I ain't the killer, honest I ain't, your worship!'

Yet this is probably the most grammatically correct option. It also has a sound pedigree. It was the accepted usage in eighteenth-century England. In modern times it is more Alf Garnett than Lord Alfred. We shun it even though it is the least incorrect option because it would make us sound common. Rules come a poor second to the image we want to convey.

What all this suggests is that change in language is Darwinian. It undergoes broadly random mutations and whether they survive depends on the environment. The environment is us. If we welcome the changes they will survive. If we do not they will perish. The question is: when should we decide whether to be hospitable or hostile, and who makes the decision on our behalf?

It Takes Two to Quango

One way to do it is to set up a quango – not that it would be called that, of course. Have you ever heard any of the great and good telling you they serve on a quango? Commissions, yes. Consultative bodies, certainly. Committees to enquire into this, that or the other. But quangos, never. It is only people who do not serve on them who use the word and when we do so there is invariably a sneer in our voice. We could instead call it an academy. Its members could adjudicate on the merits and weaknesses of proposed changes in the way we speak. Verdicts could be handed down on whether expressions such as 'innit' should be embraced or consigned to oblivion.

That is what the French do. It is hard to think of a more illustrious institution than the Académie Française, founded in 1634 to protect the French language. Its members are not so much elected as anointed by God. There was a great fuss when someone had the effrontery to put his own name forward. The impertinence of the man! Who was he, after all, but Valéry Giscard d'Estaing, a mere former President of the Republic!

Those who disapprove of the institution say it has something of the British House of Lords about it: its principal merit is that it proves the existence of life after death. And it is true that its members are so revered they are known as the 'Immortals'. Naturally, no one takes the slightest notice of their pronouncements.

They also have the General Commission on Terminology and Neology, which pronounces on the acceptability of Anglo-Saxon interlopers. But whatever these august bodies rule, in the end the French will decide for themselves what words to use. If they choose to enjoy *le rosbif* at *le weekend* while discussing problems of *le parking* and whether to buy *la stock option*, then that is what they will do and no power on earth can stop them. No Académie for us, then.

Who Can Guide Us?

If we cannot rely on the rules, then where can we turn? Well, who needs rules when we have the real, living proof of what works and what is, therefore, acceptable? We do not need some pointy-headed academic with a ribbon in his lapel or dandruff on his collar to tell us what is good language. We can read it for ourselves. And some of the very greatest literature is written in the English language. So if we need to decide what is good English we can simply turn to the works of Shakespeare and Milton, Wordsworth and Dickens. That seems to make sense – until you come across this sort of thing:

> Sweet Bassanio, my ships have all miscarried, my creditors grow cruel, my estate is very low, my bond to the Jew is forfeit; and since, in paying it, it is impossible I should live, all debts are clear'd between you and I . . .

'Between you and I'. The howler to end all howlers.

I once wrote a column for *The Times* about something of no great consequence. It would have passed unnoticed had it not been for the headline. A small diversion here, while I point out for the benefit of the uninitiated that headlines are never written by the authors of the articles but by a special breed known as sub-editors. The best of them are touched with genius. To condense a complicated story into three or four words – or even just one word that will demand the readers' attention – is a rare skill.

Of the thousands of newspaper headlines in the Falklands War, most of us remember (with admiration or loathing) only one: 'Gotcha!' It was the single word on the front page of the *Sun* – the work of what is known in the trade as the 'splash sub'. The great headlines from bygone years vary from the absurd ('General Flies Back To Front' or 'Father Of Ten Shot In Wood: Mistaken For Rabbit') to the inspired. A Hollywood newspaper known for its clever headlines used this one to tell the story of a man who escaped from a psychiatric hospital, raped a woman in a laundry and got away: 'Nut Screws Washer and Bolts'. Politically correct it was not, but those were different times.

Sub-editors are also meant to spot mistakes. A good one can save a writer's reputation; a bad one can destroy it. I can never decide whether the *Times* man who got his hands on my modest offering was out to get me or whether he was just plain ignorant. Here's what he wrote above my story about the long hours worked by the Prime Minister and me: 'Work

Comes Second for Tony and I'. The nation – or at least a very large part of it – was outraged and I spent weeks answering the letters.

So what was Shakespeare thinking about? Was it some subtle dig at the disgraceful standards of literacy among the merchant classes of sixteenth-century Venice? Presumably even then they were people who ended their correspondence with the fatuous 'assuring you of our best attention at all times'. Or did even Shakespeare make mistakes? Or does the fact that Shakespeare himself wrote this mean it isn't a mistake? Here's another writer:

London. Michaelmas term lately over, and the Lord Chancellor sitting in Lincoln's Inn Hall. Implacable November weather. As much mud in the streets, as if the waters had but newly retired from the face of the earth, and it would not be wonderful to meet a Megalosaurus, forty feet long or so, waddling like an elephantine lizard up Holborn Hill. Smoke lowering down from the chimney-pots, making a soft black drizzle with flakes of soot in it as big as full-grown snowflakes – gone into mourning, one might imagine for the death of the sun. Dogs, indistinguishable in mire. Horses, scarcely better; splashed to their very blinkers. Foot passengers, jostling one another's umbrellas . . .

No, this is not the work of Tony Blair or the many other politicians who avoid main verbs whenever possible (more of that later) but Charles Dickens. It is the opening of one of the great novels in the English language, *Bleak House*. Maybe Mr Dickens needed a good sub-editor to remind him that the rules require sentences to contain proper main verbs. Or maybe the rules are so much hooey.

Usage Rules OK?

If even the greatest writers are not bound by the rules and we have no French-style academy to lay down the law, who is to decide what is acceptable and what is not? The answer is us – all of us, one way or another. Usage rules. The way we choose to use the language is what determines what stays and what goes – and that's the only way it can be. We are the final court of appeal. There can be no other.

That sounds like a cop-out because there are so many people who worry about what they see as the deterioration of the language and want something done about it. But what it means is that there are no weapons in this battle other than argument and persuasion. We simply have to convince people that one way of using words is better than another.

It is not good enough to say: 'You must do this because of the "rules".' Rules are there to be broken unless they can be justified by reason. Only then should they carry weight. Miss Smythe's rules were mostly good, not because she said so, but because they could be shown to have some value. Caring about language is not a form of sado-masochism. So we argue our corner, example by example, knowing that usage is the final court of appeal. The best we can do is try to sway the argument – as much by our own usage as anything.

Win Some ... Lose Some

This means we have to reconcile ourselves from the outset to disappointments. A changing language is full of richness, novelty and fun. There will be regrets for some of what has passed and what our efforts and influence have been unable to save. I don't know how we came to lose this:

She is with child.

Isn't it a delightful expression, soft and gentle and redolent of the most intimate relationship? And we threw it out for this hard, technical-sounding Latinate phrase:

'She's pregnant.'

The first phrase conveys the sense of two humans linked as one. The second removes the growing baby from the thought. There is a lot to be said for beauty and emotion.

We can, if we wish, hold out for our own personal favourites and keep using the words and phrases we enjoy. I detest the word 'slash' in website addresses. When I read out the *Today* programme address on the air I always say 'stroke' – an altogether more elegant word. Many people write (never email) to me to say they prefer it too. Many more think I'm slightly bonkers. If the world has moved on and we do not move with it, we are labelled eccentrics – or worse.

I don't suppose there is anyone left who still insists on it, but I would love to meet someone who continues the old English usage of 'thou'. I know 'thee', 'tha' and 'thissen' are used in Yorkshire, but that's dialect. Delightful and important though it is, it's not quite what I'm talking about. 'Thou' would be a wonderful way to distinguish between intimates and acquaintances.

Of course in English it's absurdly archaic and it will never catch on again, but it works on the Continent in other modern languages. The French have '*tu*' and '*vous*' and the Germans have '*du*' and '*sie*' and there is a real point to this. It provides a way of conveying the closeness or formality of a relationship. It might even be effective for interviewing politicians – especially those who don't really know me from Adam but insist on calling me 'John' at every opportunity. I suppose they think it suggests to the listener that we are old pals and it's all just a bit of fun really.

The other advantage of the two forms of address is that it is useful for putting people in their place. Shortly after he became President of France, François Mitterrand was asked by one of his oldest confidants whether he minded if he continued to '*tu-toi*' him. With magnificent hauteur the great man replied: 'You may, *si vous voulez*.' I suppose I could try a variation of that on *Today*.

Usage, then, is the final arbiter. That is how it should be in a democracy because language is to democracy what water is to life. For too long people who care about language have allowed themselves to be represented as authoritarian monsters wanting to impose their views on everyone else. Some do and they will fail. Many more are just worried about the way things are going and would like to feel their voices are being heard. They want to be able to engage in the argument and try to have some influence in the battle over usage. Let battle now be joined.

CHAPTER FIVE

Writing Ain't Speaking

There is bad writing and there is seriously bad writing. It's easy to poke fun at the hideous stuff that pours from the word-processors of a thousand bureaucrats every day. I did it at the start of this book. I could fill every page with it if I thought you could take it. The culprits might argue that it is unfair to ridicule them. They might even have a point. Their job is to run the country, not to write elegant prose. I would argue that they would make a better job of running the country if we, the poor souls who have to observe their regulations, could understand them. But at least they have an excuse of sorts. There is no excuse for this:

> At last, at the turn of the century, IT has finally matured into adjectives such as 'cheap' and 'easy to use', with the tsunami of applications and knock-on implications it has for our lives.

That is an extract from a book described by Bryan Appleyard as 'the worst written book I have ever reviewed'. Mr Appleyard – himself a first-rate journalist and stylish writer – has reviewed many books in his time. Is he exaggerating? Well, here are a few more samples so you may judge for yourself:

These doom-laden imaginings need a pinch of salt. Setting aside the obvious precaution of not volunteering for a brain implant, even if the opportunity for psychokinesis was too valuable to pass over the direct implanting of thoughts would still not necessarily be feasible.

Follow that, did you? Possibly not. How about something simpler?

Instead you will surrender wholesale to the once-occasional passive reception of the senses, interacting with and to the ebb and flow of inputs and outputs from all other fellow beings via your cyber world.

Did I say simpler? Let's try another book then:

This consciousness of risk is as powerful in regard to human relations as they are in relation to new technology and the environment.

This comes from the same book:

According to Steinem, steps designed to raise self-esteem would both empower the individual as well as women.

So does this:

After registering their child as needing special need, a protracted process of negotiation ensues before statementing a student as entitled to special support.

And this:

The diseasing of so-called negative emotions distract attention from the fact that maybe it is the conditions that gave rise to them that needs to be cured.

I know what you're thinking. Anyone can get it wrong. Show me the person who has never written a lousy sentence and I'll show you the child who has yet to learn the alphabet. We all make mistakes. My own writing is littered with them. But the stuff I have just quoted is not just wrong: it is impenetrable. It is so dense and clumsy that most of us would prefer to spend an hour reading Proust in Japanese than wade through it. And this is sad, because both writers have so much to say.

When you talk to them, as I have done many times, you are struck by their originality. The first was Susan Greenfield, professor of pharmacology at Oxford. She is so celebrated in her field that she is now Baroness Greenfield. If it were not for the fact that she wears very short skirts and has a great talent for publicity (no bad thing for a scientist) she would almost certainly have been admitted to the Royal Society. There is no more august body than that.

The other author was Frank Furedi, professor of sociology at the University of Kent. His thoughts on our society's tendency to 'cultivate vulnerability', as he puts it, stimulate and provoke. He deserves to be read. But why make it so difficult? What happens when they sit at their word-processors? What strange mechanism takes over and turns their prose into the literary equivalent of lumpy porridge? They can think clearly. They know a lot. In conversation they speak with enthusiasm and passion. And yet they produce sentences on paper that make you run for cover.

It's not like making soup. The cook has all the right ingredients, chops them up, boils them with some nice herbs and then tips it all into the liquidiser. Result: wonderful soup. Some people use the same approach with writing, hoping it will produce a similar result. It won't.

The Loose Tooth

The first point to be made is that writing is not the same as speaking. Spoken English is full of mistakes that pass us by without our ever really noticing them. Transcribing spontaneous conversation, then reading it from the printed page is a revealing – and cruel – business. We do it in broadcasting to make it easier to edit interviews.

You talk to some politicians for twenty minutes and then you get the transcript back. It can be a nightmare digging out a usable thirty seconds. What sounded perfectly coherent looks, on the printed page, like gibberish. In all my years of interviewing I can recall only a tiny handful of politicians whose transcripts read as though they had been written. I suppose Enoch Powell must have made the odd howler, but I can't remember one. He spoke with a precision that was chilling. Normal people slip up all the time. We make the most elementary errors – often confusing singular and plural.

This is how the former chairman of the BBC, Sir Christopher Bland, described the protests that followed the sacking of Greg Dyke:

'The extent of those demonstrations show that . . .'

You'd have to have a sharp ear to spot that it was

ungrammatical, but ungrammatical it was. It is the same with this:

'I'll stay as long as the Prime Minister and the Home Secretary wants me to.'

That was the immigration minister, Beverley Hughes. In fairness, she had a lot on her mind when she committed her little solecism. It turned out that the Prime Minister did not want her to stay very long at all and she was out of her job the next day.

I hear myself doing this all the time:

'The government's in trouble because they . . .'

But it's only when you see these things in print that they jump out at you. This sort of thing, spotted in *The Times* by an irritated reader:

. . . the raw power of the performances by Gwyneth Paltrow and Daniel Craig touch nerves that . . .

The same reader seems to make a habit of latching onto these things in *The Times*. Here's another from the same edition:

Research has shown that the risks involved in taking

HRT, other than for two or three years . . . is not justified.

The point is not just that bad grammar jolts us more in written English than in spoken English. In print it can also confuse us about what is meant, even when the same words in colloquial speech do not have that effect. That's probably because we have time to think about it when we see it on a page. We can worry away at it, in the same way that the tongue keeps returning to a loose tooth.

We all have our least favourite. Mine is the misplaced 'only' as in: 'He was only the Pope for a short time when he was shot.' Now that is a very interesting notion. 'Only' the Pope. What a pathetic achievement! Surely he could have done more with his life. Become God, perhaps? It is a modest little word, but 'only' can do wonders for a sentence. That's why I got so excited when my small son managed to put it in the right place – even if it was more by accident than design. In this case, 'only' was meant to emphasise how recently John Paul had become Pope before the assassination attempt.

Sue Lawley may not know it but at least one of her listeners hurls abuse at the radio when she asks her castaway on the desert island: 'And if you could only take one record . . . ?'

I'm with my correspondent on this one. 'Only

one record' would not sound particularly pompous or pedantic and would have the virtue of being grammatical. Not that I intend telling her. I'm still waiting for my own invitation to appear on the programme (a *far* greater honour than the knighthood that I've not been offered either) and would hate to do anything to queer my pitch.

Take this simple sentence:

Tony Blair listens to Gordon Brown's advice.

Now add the word 'only'. There are several places it could sensibly fit. In each case the new sentence would produce a radically different meaning. It could mean Blair listens to Brown and does nothing or that he listens to nobody but Brown or that no one but Blair listens to Brown. One little word in the wrong place and you rewrite the most important relationship in British politics since Cromwell had the royal head chopped off.

In the catalogue of misplaced words 'only' suffers more than most. But you can play the game with many more.

Sloppiness Abounds

The Bill is not thought to include any further concessions.

That sentence came from the *Birmingham Post* and I dislike almost everything about it. What's wrong with 'more' instead of 'further'? Why does 'bill' get a capital letter? Above all, why is 'not' in the wrong place? What the writer wants to say is simple enough: 'It is thought the bill will include no more concessions.' Why doesn't he say it?

Here's another whinge:

The person's name cannot be revealed for legal reasons.

You can spend happy hours speculating on the reasons that *would* allow the person to be named. To make Max Clifford a great deal of money, perhaps, or simply because the person would very much like to see his name in the headlines. A simple rearrangement solves the problem:

For legal reasons, the person's name cannot be revealed.

There are other reasons for holding back names. An old colleague of mine, Bob Friend, occasionally had a liquid lunch before presenting the news for Sky. On one occasion he was half-way through his presenting stint when he was handed some Reuters copy breaking the news that a plane had crashed in East Africa, killing everyone on board. The dead included two presidents with names that were unpronounceable even to the stone cold sober. Bob realised he'd never get away with it. Having announced that two presidents had been killed he ended: 'Their names will not be released until their next of kin have been informed.' Now that's a real newsman at work.

Something else we do in speech all the time is confuse 'may' and 'might'. We interchange them routinely. Mostly it doesn't matter. Occasionally it does. One Radio Four listener complained to me about the announcer who trailed a programme that would tell us 'how Martina Navratilova may never have won her Wimbledon championships'.

Now that's odd. You watched her do it. Perhaps they got the scores wrong and have only just discovered it. Unlikely. Perhaps some legal challenge was being mounted to prove that she was really a man and should not have been competing with the ladies. Even that is unlikely. What the announcer meant was that she *might* never have won all those championships because she almost chose to do something else with her life. I have a sneaking feeling that we rather like using 'may' because it is vaguely posh – rather like 'shall' instead of 'will'. 'Shall James call the guests for dinner, Papa?'

The Danger of Dangling

In every large company that deals with 'consumers' (a silly word: we all 'consume') there is a department dedicated to customer service or, increasingly and even sillier, 'customer experience'. If things go wrong its purpose is to find as many ingenious ways as possible of persuading you that it is not the company's fault but your own. Occasionally it will admit it made a mistake and offer you compensation.

If, for instance, your luxurious holiday villa on a sun-kissed coast surrounded by exotic palm trees turns out to be a filthy shack without running water next to the cement works and directly beneath the airport flight path, they will offer you a ten-pound voucher to be used against your next holiday. This is one of the ways customer-service departments conspire to cause you maximum irritation. The other is to send you unsolicited letters.

Probably the worst culprits are financial services companies (that word 'service' again) who want you to add another plastic card to the two dozen already bulging from your wallet. If you already have one of their cards they will try to sell you another 'service'.

Occasionally you might be caught off guard and actually read one of the letters. After it has spelt your name wrongly it will begin with something like this:

As one of our cardholders, I should like to . . .

This is known as a dangling clause. It should be a hanging offence. For a moment you are puzzled. Why should this peculiar being known as a Customer Experience Director want to tell you that he uses one of his company's own cards? Then you realise he means *you*. So why did he phrase his letter to suggest otherwise? It is one of life's great mysteries. The curious thing is that it is actually more difficult to write sentences with dangling clauses than it is to get it right.

'Being a not very bright man and ill at ease with the English language, Tony Blair likes to explain things to George Bush in simple terms.' Funny, maybe, but it won't do. However much we muddle things up in speech, when we write them down we should attach the clause to its subject. Otherwise this sort of thing happens:

Surrounded by barbed wire, armed soldiers guarded the prisoners from watchtowers.

How very uncomfortable for the soldiers. That was sent to me by one of my many correspondents. I've just heard this on the radio:

> Driving in from the airport, the flags were fluttering proudly.

What accomplished flags they must have been.

I Beg to Differ

If you think this all far too pernickety and that we won't really go wrong if we simply write as we speak, try listening to a football manager talking about the weekend game:

> 'Well, we're hoping for a result on Saturday, Gary.'

No, he's not. He's hoping to win. There's going to be a result come what may. Even a draw is a result.
But this is worse:

> 'We're anticipating a result on Saturday, Gary.'

Here is where a true pedant could go to town. I like to think that if I were Gary Richardson and someone said that to me I would demand clarification. Something along these lines:

'Does that mean that because you expect the expected to happen and the game to be played you are taking some action in advance which presupposes the fact?'

Perhaps not. I suspect Gary's job is safe. But there is a serious point here. Respecting the difference between words is not about being pedantic or pompous or even perfectionist. It just means we can express ourselves more clearly. And surely that matters when we write or when scripts are read across the airwaves. A 'result' is not the same as a 'win'. 'To anticipate' is not the same as 'to expect' – just as 'to prevaricate' is not the same as 'to procrastinate' and 'to presume' is not the same as 'to assume'. 'Disinterested' means something different from 'uninterested' and that's that: it always has and it always should because it is not easy to find another word that means quite the same. That is why I gave Alastair Campbell a hard time for getting it wrong. Getting it wrong is, to labour the point, unacceptable rather than intolerable.

I had letters after a BBC reporter said this about the terrorist attacks on the Madrid railway station:

'To begin with, people did not realise the enormity of the event.'

I'm sure they did. An enormity is a moral outrage, which is what it certainly was. What they did not realise to begin with was that there had been so many bombs.

One woman wrote to me about forms that ask what her gender, rather than her sex, is:

> I write 'neuter', on the grounds that this is more or less what I score on psychometric masculinity/ femininity tests.

Quite right too: I bet that gets them baffled. Gender and sex are not the same thing at all.

You may think some of these distinctions are fairly subtle, but often we say one thing when we intend to say exactly the opposite. 'Begging' the question could hardly be more different from 'raising' the question, yet we do it all the time. To 'beg the question' is to make an assumption: it 'begs' to be challenged. Yes, I know everyone will understand what we mean, but that's not the point. Using it wrongly means its real value has been lost for ever, which is a pity.

The importance of all this really cannot be under-estimated. Except, of course, that it can be – and often is. I guarantee that the next time you read or hear that construction it will be used incorrectly. It takes only a second to work out that I should have written 'cannot be *over*estimated'.

Inflation

We lose good words when we use them wrongly but we also lose them when they become devalued. We blunt their meanings. The linguist Geoffrey Hughes calls this 'verbicide', which produces 'zombie' words. 'Hero' is one. Can it really be the case that we have so many more heroes these days than in the past? It seems unlikely, given that most of us have never heard a shot fired in anger and the closest we get to real danger is risking a heart-attack by stuffing ourselves with hamburgers. But next time you have a few hours to spare, count the number of heroes you come across in a week's newspapers. Mostly they are on the sports pages.

You become a hero in football by doing something that carries no risk (except possibly jeopardising your vast salary) and for which you have been trained since you were old enough to lace your own boots: kicking a ball into a net. This is something I cannot do and I envy those who can. But it does not make them heroes. Skilled footballers, yes. Heroes, no.

You might think that heroes remain heroes – but not in sport. They quickly become villains if the ball does not go into the net – as David Beckham found to his cost in Portugal in 2004. Lawrence Dallaglio was a hero when England won the Rugby World Cup. A few months later, according to the *Sun*, he was one of a number of gutless failures who had 'let down the best sports fans in the world'. I wonder how one qualifies for that. And as for Tim Henman, he has switched from heroic to hopeless more often than he has served a double fault.

Nor do nurses necessarily become heroes (or even angels) the moment they pin on their little upside-down watches. It is not heroic to do your job properly – unless you are a traffic warden or possibly a teacher in one of those schools where the kiddies carry knives instead of ballpoints and pop into a lesson occasionally to keep their clients supplied with skunk. You need to be either brave or foolhardy to try teaching fifteen-year-olds who really do not want to be taught. Or possibly suicidal.

'Tragic' is, if anything, even more abused. It is tragic when a penalty is missed; tragic when a pop star wannabe (now *there*'s a good new word) fails to impress the judge on a television show; tragic when a factory closes and people lose their jobs. There are dozens of words to describe this sort of thing: unfortunate, disappointing, worrying. But tragic? No. That is a word we should reserve for big things.

'Shame' is on this list too. It has a clear meaning but has been so devalued it now means merely 'regrettable'. 'Name and shame' is one of those phrases that should be tied up in a sack and dumped in the deepest ocean. Even 'pity' is overused – often by me. Once it was a powerful word. Now it is puny. We say it with a shrug. That's a pity – or is it a shame? Why don't we settle for 'regrettable'?

Further down the list is this sort of thing: 'Jonny Wilkinson kicked an incredible penalty.' No, he didn't. He kicks so many penalties (or was doing at the time of writing) that they are all too credible. It is exactly what we expect of him. The problem is how to describe one that is better than most. 'Excellent'? Well, maybe, but it's a bit flat and dull. 'Admirable' does the job perfectly – we all admire great skill – but it sounds pompous. It's like 'agreeable' to describe a pleasant meal. You rather feel that you don't quite qualify to use it unless you went to a decent public school. Odd, but there it is.

The new(ish) word is 'phenomenal' – which is about as unsuited to the task as it gets, although it is marginally less ridiculous than the other contender, 'awesome'. I once heard a salad dressing described as awesome. I wonder what that makes the Victoria Falls in full flood or the Beethoven Quartets.

'Serious' has been flogged to death in recent years. Any association with its original meaning seems to be disappearing. Russian oligarchs are 'seriously' rich. Manchester United or Chelsea Football Clubs have 'serious' money to spend. My old colleague Martyn Lewis was on a food programme talking about a 'serious' mousse. I very much doubt he was being ironic.

It has happened with 'obscene'. The original meaning has been eroded over the years and it is now used to express general disapproval – sometimes with a twinge of envy. But a touch of wit and irony can help redeem a word's meaning. George Clooney proved as much when he turned to Catherine Zeta-Jones in the film *Intolerable Cruelty* and remarked, 'Obscene wealth becomes you.' So, indeed, it does.

Please Don't Let Me Be Misunderstood

The reason precision matters is simple enough: we want our meaning to get across. There are exceptions: there is sometimes an equally strong urge to be ambiguous. When Maynard Keynes became the most famous economist in the world he received many letters. They were often from ambitious young students who hoped to become the great man's *protégés*. They would include their theses with the request that he read them and return them with his comments. Keynes, it is said, had a standard reply:

Thank you so much for sending me your thesis. I
shall lose no time in reading it.
Yours sincerely,
J. M. Keynes

Now that is ambiguity with a purpose. Actors do
it all the time when they are required to praise a colleague's performance. No actor ever tells another how
dreadful he was, even if the entire audience had fallen
asleep during the performance, walked out or hurled
abuse. It is said that the unfortunate actor who played
Anne Frank was so awful in her starring role that,
when the Gestapo arrived at her house to search it,
the entire audience shouted as one, 'She's in the attic!'

But actors dare not do that to each other. They
might get the same honesty in return one day. They
must, at all costs, preserve the myth. And they have
developed a whole range of responses for the fraught
opening-night party. One of my favourites is 'Darling! I can't tell you how wonderful you were!' I also
like 'Darling! Words simply fail me!' Or the simple
but deadly 'Darling! What can I say?' Ambiguity
can be useful.

But mostly we want our meaning to get across.
Once again speech gives us a freedom to be lax that
is not available to the written word. If you were
discussing the most famous man in the world with
a friend in the pub he might say:

'There's no question that Beckham had an affair.'

His expression and emphasis would tell you what he meant. If there were a knowing smile he would mean one thing but if he seemed outraged he would mean something else. In print the sentence would be ambiguous. You would need one other word to clear it up:

> 'There's no question but that David Beckham had an affair'

(or 'didn't have' as the case may be).

You might say this about his appearance: 'His hair could do with cutting badly . . .' but you'd never put it into print. It is risky to transfer the freedom enjoyed by spoken English to the written word.

The late Tory politician, Alan Clark, was rich, funny, snobbish, a rather unpleasant man and a great diarist. He was also a compulsive womaniser. Imagine this being written about his long-suffering wife, Jane:

She hated him carrying on with other women.

Does it mean she hated him for carrying on with other women? Or does it mean that she continued to love him and it was his 'carrying on' that she hated? It would have been easy to avoid the ambiguity. The writer could have inserted a comma.

She hated him, carrying on with other women.

That slight pause, enforced by the comma, would have made it clear. It was Clark himself she hated. Or the writer could have added one small word:

She hated him for carrying on with other women.

Again, it is perfectly clear what she hated: her philandering husband. But what if the writer were trying to say the opposite? Well, then, all that was needed was to change one letter. Instead of 'him' it should be 'his':

She hated his carrying on with other women.

The pedants will say this proves the value of unbreakable rules. Doesn't *everyone* know that 'carrying on' is a gerund, which means that the possessive is required? Well, actually, no, they don't. Nor do they need to. All they need do is apply a bit more care in their writing than they would need to do in speech and read the sentence back after it has been written. If it leaves room for ambiguity, it is wrong. But there are few rules that are truly unbreakable.

Bad Habits

As you will have noticed, I habitually start sentences with conjunctions and end them with prepositions. I can't see anything wrong with that. Both 'and' and 'but' are useful words with which to begin a sentence – or even to end one with. 'However' instead of 'but' is clumsy. Any word that requires a pair of commas to surround it before it is allowed out in public should stay at home. Nor do I mind occasionally reading 'don't' instead of 'do not'. Spoken English uses it all the time. Avoiding it can sound stilted. I am even happy to write sentences with no verb. Honestly. But there are limits. Confusing 'I' and 'me' breaks the limit, which is why I want to return to it.

You do not need to know that one is nominative and the other accusative. All you need to know is why they should not be mixed up. When a semi-literate yob says, 'Me and my mate kicked the sh..t out of them wankers,' it is what you expect him to say. There is disgust, but no great shock. If a vicar says it you are surprised – though not as surprised as you might once have been. But when people who write books about language break the rule you are entitled to curl your lip – especially if they cannot blame a sub-editor.

In a column for the *Sunday Times* I described a

conversation I'd had with a researcher from that deeply silly programme *I'm a Celebrity . . . Get Me Out of Here*. She had asked me, bizarrely, to be one of the 'celebrities'. I accepted but, I wrote, there was one condition:

> I would do it only if they signed up Tony Blair as well. There was a small pause and she thanked me kindly and hung up. Pity really. We could have had some fascinating conversations, Tony and me, as we put poisonous snakes down each other's underpants or whatever you're meant to do.

I was deliberately using the colloquial when I wrote 'Tony and me'. I might have got away with it – just – had I not done something similar later in the same article. Perhaps I'd got into the habit by then. This time I was writing about reporting the campaign for the presidential election in the United States in 1976: 'Nobody was more surprised than me when he actually won.'

In my final column for the newspaper I wrote this:

> The waters will close over my head and better writers than me will grace this page in the months and years to come.

Well, I was asking for it and it happened. Here's a typical reaction: 'They couldn't be much worse, could they, Mr Humphrys? At least they might observe the rules of grammar.'

Fair enough, I suppose. But many readers would have thought it pedantic had I written 'more sur-prised than I'. Others, I suspect, would have said, 'What's all the fuss about? It really doesn't matter.' But most would have hesitated to venture an opinion one way or another – too unsure of themselves when they stumble into this grammatical territory. I think it has a lot to do with wanting to *appear* to use the language correctly.

It is class as much as grammar that makes the I/ me debate such an interesting one. Naturally the Queen is to blame. We all know that 'My husband and I' is correct and we all know that it is pro-foundly ignorant to say, 'Me and the missus'. So what many educated people do if they don't know the rules is opt for safe ground. And you can't get safer than the Queen, can you? Hence we get this sort of letter appearing in the newspapers.

Dear Sir
It is a matter of deep concern to my wife and I . . .

It is so obviously wrong and the test could scarcely be simpler. Can anyone imagine writing 'It is a matter of deep concern to I'? So let that be an end to it. But it won't be. For every sad case who confuses subject with object there is another who tries to cover his confusion by substituting an even posher version. It ends up like this:

It is a matter of deep concern to my wife and myself . . .

It gets even worse. One woman swore in a letter to me that she had heard Tony Blair say the following:

'Myself and the Prime Minister of India intend to ensure . . .'

Hard to believe, but there it is. She wrote to her building society and their reply included this glorious question:

Do you bank with ourselves?

To which the correct response should be: 'Not any longer I don't.' What, in the name of Her Britannic Majesty and all that is holy, is wrong with 'us' or 'me' or 'I'?

Remember Hobbes

There is no point in simply moaning that people have stopped learning grammar and the rules of writing. People who haven't had the good fortune to learn, but still want to write properly, need a bit of advice. Perhaps the best is: remember Thomas Hobbes.

Robert Burchfield begins his book, *The English Language*, with a quotation from Hobbes's *Leviathan*:

> A man that seeketh precise truth, had need to remember what every name he uses stands for; and to place it accordingly; or else he will find himselfe entangled in words, as a bird in lime-twiggs; the more he struggles, the more belimed.

In other words: take care with words or you will become belimed. The sad thing is that the rules did a lot of that 'taking care' for us. Without them, we have to work it out for ourselves. Fortunately, plenty of people do and they kick up whenever they read something they deplore. In the battle to influence usage we have to keep doing that until we think the game is up. And even then we can go on writing our own English as we think it should be written.

There is probably a law somewhere out there that

says no one may write a book about the use of English without referring to the 'less/fewer' debate. I had promised myself I would try to avoid the temptation, but why? Of all the things that give a jolt to people who are attentive to language, the use of 'less' when it should be 'fewer' is near the top of the list.

Pragmatists say it is a pointless debate. Either people know what's right or they don't – and, more to the point, don't really care one way or the other. Even if they do care, nothing happens. One of my correspondents complained to the manager of her local Marks & Spencer because the checkout sign said, 'Five items or less'. The manager shrugged and said, 'Oh, it's a corporate thing' – clearly the business equivalent of 'I was only obeying orders'.

On the other hand, when William Safire made a fuss about the same thing in the column he writes for the *New York Times* the supermarket concerned changed its policy. And more recently M&S seems to have mended its ways too. So something can be done – if you care.

The reason for the distinction is interesting. Different societies sort the countable from the un-countable in different ways. One of the earliest sociolinguists, the American Benjamin Lee Whorf, made a study of the Hopi Amerindians of Arizona and noticed that they did not count things as we do because they viewed the world differently. There was much less for them to count because they did not see everything as individual objects, as we tend to do. A later sociolinguist, J. A. Lucy, discovered that some Mexicans regarded only animate beings as existing in the plural and thus capable of being counted.

Here Are the News

We make it more complicated. Some things may be plural; others may not. Bread is bread – no matter how much of it there may be – but loaves are loaves. Water is singular but lakes are plural. Sugar is singular. Imagine saying: 'Would you mind passing the sugars?' If you did, you'd never pass one of David Blunkett's English-language courses for foreigners who want to live here.

Some things seem to pass between the singular and the plural. I suspect 'media' is one of those words that is gradually becoming a singular noun because we use it almost always to describe a single entity. Some say we should not mess about with words like that. Once a plural, always a plural. I don't agree. People would think I'd gone potty if I announced this at eight o'clock in the morning on Radio Four:

'The news are read by Peter Donaldson.'

Yet there was a time when that would have been regarded as the correct usage. In 1861 Queen Victoria wrote to the King of the Belgians to say:

> The news from Austria are very sad and make one very anxious.

But if you can count things, you end up with a number. If you can't, you end up with some other way of expressing the amount. And that, of course, takes us back to 'less' and 'fewer'. 'Few' is a word applicable only to what is countable. You can't count sugar. So this is not a subjective preference. It exists because the world is divided up into the countable and the uncountable.

Mostly the error goes in one direction. No one says, 'I'd like fewer water in my whisky, please'. But no less a figure than a former Chief Inspector for Schools, Mike Tomlinson, used 'less' when he meant 'fewer' on my programme. Who will teach the teachers, eh? The same process is going on with the use of 'number' and 'amount'. You won't hear people say, 'The number of rubbish piling up in the street is becoming unsightly,' but you will hear them say, 'The amount of people who drop litter is appalling.'

It's not only the linguistic rule being broken here. There is something unpleasant in talking about people as an 'amount'. Remember that loathsome picture of Iraqi prisoners piled in a heap for the amusement of their American jailers? There may be some sense behind what we choose to count and what we don't, especially when it comes to human beings.

I can think of only one exception to the general rule of countable versus uncountable. Here's an example: 'The majority of the Prime Minister's time is spent in meetings.' It doesn't work. Time is indivisible. You could talk about the majority of hours or minutes if you wished, but that would be silly and pretentious when 'most' exists to do the job.

Nonsense

I wonder if this bothers you:

Both sides agreed to resume negotiations.

The verb 'agree' requires two distinct agents to be in play at the time. 'Both' loses them in a collective blur. It should be

The two sides agreed.

The same problem arises with this:

Both sides criticised each other.

It should be 'Each side criticised the other'. Again, you may say: so what? The meaning is clear enough and that is what matters. But if you pay close attention to the language it's the sort of thing that gives you a jolt.

If you disagree I would expect you to say, 'That's nonsense.' Nowadays you might very well say 'a nonsense' instead. It is becoming fashionable to add the indefinite article. This is another curious business. Turning a notion into a thing is common – the posh word for the process is 'reification' – and I want to come back to its more important effects later. But since we are on the business of delivering jolts to people who worry about the language, let's take a look at it.

It seems like a case of wanting to add bogus authority to an opinion. If something we disagree with can be classified in relation to some existing category, it sounds somehow more official. Talking about 'a nonsense' is then on a par with talking about a fallacy, a tautology, or a contradiction in terms. But it's nonsense. Are we going to start talking about 'a drivel' or 'a bunkum'? Nonsense is nonsense.

The best antidote to this misuse I can think of is to summon up the image of someone who characteristically uses the notion a lot. Think of Lewis Carroll's Red Queen or Margaret Thatcher in her prime and you will hear it used peremptorily and properly: 'Nonsense!'

CHAPTER SIX

Harsh Words

I have appeared on stage a few times with Barry Humphries. If it is a mistake for actors to play alongside children and animals it is madness for people like me to work with people like him – unless we enjoy humiliation. That's not because he is cruel. Quite the contrary, he's a delightful man. But he is a brilliant comic whose genius lies in exposing the frailty and vanity of human nature. You work with such people at your peril. He apologised to me once for making me look an idiot. I had tried talking to him off-stage as though he were Barry Humphries when he was dressed as Dame Edna. It was Dame Edna who replied – crushingly. As he told me later, 'When I'm dressed as her I *am* her. I can't do it any other way.' Exactly so. It was my fault, not his.

His strengths are not only his inventive mind and his acute observation of human nature, but also his ear for language. You may remember Dame Edna (by her own admission a truly caring person) talking about her dependants. Her aged mother was in a 'twilight home'. She would visit her occasionally for an evening stroll 'down to the electric fence'. Her husband, Norm, was on a life-support system. Dame Edna faced a moral dilemma. Was it her duty to keep him alive or should she be thinking of the planet and turn off the machine to save the electricity? Ruminating on this quandary she produced this immortal line:

> 'You know, possums, you can overcare for an institutionalised loved one.'

That sort of thing produces some very uneasy laughter. What a vicious world is created in that one sentence. 'Overcare' is a hateful word. I'm waiting for it to find its way into the lexicon of some bureaucrat worried about his budget. 'Institutionalised' is one we have been using for some years now. It encapsulates the whole ghastly business of seeing people not as individual human beings but as inputs in a process.

Language betrays how we see the world. When we stop talking of people as people, with all their frailty and weaknesses, their warmth and humanity, we expose a hardening in ourselves – or, more accurately, a hardening that our culture encourages in us. It is surprising what adding '-ise' can do. Many people hate the idea that you can create a verb from a noun (or, sometimes, an adjective) simply by adding those few letters.

When the first edition of *The Complete Plain Words* by Sir Ernest Gowers was published in 1954 it warned against the use of 'publicise, finalise, casualise and diarise'. David Crystal is the doyen of those clever people who study the use of language and he concludes that there is little point in complaining: it seems to make no difference.

> In the third edition of Gowers' book, published in 1986, the objections to *publicise* and the others are no longer cited. Instead new -ise words are mentioned as currently attracting opposition, such as *prioritise* and *routinise*.

Ah, well, notch up one small victory: we haven't started 'routinising'. Not yet anyway.

I'm not sure I agree with Professor Crystal when he suggests there is no point in kicking up about all this. Clearly it depends on the word. 'Publicise' is useful. We'd struggle to manage without it – especially now that gaining publicity seems to be the sole ambition of about half the population. Why else would they want to appear on *Big Brother*? But 'hospitalise' is a thoroughly unpleasant creation. I can't see that

'George has been hospitalised'

has any advantage over

'George has been admitted to hospital'

The first version saves a few letters, it's true, but it removes something from George. If he is merely 'admitted to hospital' he remains George. But to be 'hospitalised' suggests a transformation of some kind. He is depersonalised – or dehumanised, which is, of course, another word that has undergone the same treatment.

The hospital itself is a victim of this linguistic process. A hospital is a complex organism. If it functions well it is because of its mix of human skills, knowledge and care. To reduce that whole healing process into something that 'hospitalises' is to turn a living institution into an impersonal production line.

Let's Impact

Sticking a suffix on to a noun is one way of hardening up the language. Another way is not to bother with the suffix at all, just to use the noun as a verb. Will Hutton wrote in the *Observer* that most people shop and 'recreate' within eight miles of their homes. I don't *think* he means it in the sense of creating something anew. Children 'truant' rather than 'play truant'. Civil servants are 'tasked' by their political masters to do things, rather than 'given a task'. That's typical of the hardness, the ugliness, of this usage. If the boss 'gives' someone a task, there is at least a courtesy about it. Being 'tasked' loses that.

In a technical context it makes sense to turn nouns into verbs. Before computers arrived to help and torment us, we talked about 'gaining access' to things. In computer-speak it would seem odd to gain access to our files, so we 'access' them. The question is whether we want that impersonal process to apply to people. I am waiting to hear divorce courts ringing to the sound of fathers 'accessing' their children. It's only a matter of time. Indeed the process has already begun. Here is no less a figure than the Lord Chief Justice, Lord Woolf, posing a rhetorical question:

> 'What is the use of courts if you cannot access them?'

Quite so, my lord, but what is the use of language if you cannot allow it to breathe a little? That, by the way, was not meant to be rhetorical.

Technology has also given us 'interface' as a verb and it, too, has spread into common use. We even talk now about people 'interfacing' with each other. Hideous. And what does it mean? Talking to each other, maybe? The BBC 'showcases' programmes these days. Wasn't 'showcase' once a noun? This kind of thing catches on quickly. Here's another one I saw in the blurb for a new book:

A bruised and cathartic debut, *Brass* mainlines us into a new and shocking world of female sexuality.

I puzzle over how a debut can be bruised and cathartic. I boggle at a new and shocking world of female sexuality. But I shudder at being mainlined into it all. Might it be addictive? I wonder.

As I write this I have a letter on my desk from someone at the Food Standards Agency asking me to take part in a survey they are conducting. The letter tells me my answers will be 'anonymised'. I think I shall tell them not to expect my co-operation because I have been antagonised.

The thing about real verbs is that they move. They are fluid. Journalists like verbs because they want to carry their readers along with them. With too many nouns sentences become leaden. That's one of the reasons why German sounds so heavy. It includes huge compound nouns that plant themselves in the middle of a sentence like an occupying force, with the verb hanging on grimly at the end. This is how Mark Twain put it:

Whenever the literary German dives into a sentence, that is the last you are going to see of him till he emerges on the other side of the Atlantic with his verb in his mouth.

In English, verbs can refresh a sentence any time they are needed – but not if they earned their crust as nouns in an earlier life. Some seriously weird ones are entering the vocabulary. Digby Jones runs the Confederation of British Industry. He is that rare specimen: a businessman who uses simple language and keeps an eye open for new absurdities. Here's one he came up with. It's the response you get if you try to fix an appointment with a busy man:

'Sorry, my diary's fully scoped right now.'

Fully scoped, eh? There's probably an entire thesis to be written on how that one came about. When and why did 'progress' become a verb – as in 'Let's progress this development'? Probably about the same time as 'impact': 'This will impact the ongoing scenario.' Or maybe the upcoming scenario.

Composite words like 'ongoing' and 'upcoming' are not only ugly: they are redundant. If the sentence is in the present tense the activity is obviously current. If it is in the future tense it has yet to happen. Some compound words present more subtle problems. Try this modest experiment. Say the following sentence aloud:

He was fundraising for the Oxfam appeal.

Now say this one aloud:

He was raising funds for the Oxfam appeal.

I'll bet that in the first sentence you put the emphasis on 'fund'. The word 'raising' was lost. In the second there was equal emphasis on 'raising' and 'funds'. The rhythm of the sentence allowed the emphasis to fall in the right places. Real verbs attach themselves to their subject. In the second sentence you hear 'He is raising' before you discover what it might be. The composite 'fundraising' takes you straight to the object, shifting the focus from the subject to the process that is being carried out. This has a distancing effect.

So does the choice of certain words. Here is what President Bush had to say at a news conference after a meeting with the Egyptian president:

'I'm grateful for the President's support as Iraq moves to democracy.'

I lie. That's what he should have said. What he actually said was:

'I'm grateful for the President's support as Iraq transitions to democracy.'

Why would he do that? It could be because he often speaks as though English were his second language – but no man who can coin a word such as 'mis-underestimate' should be treated lightly. Or it could be that he was not (to use an Americanism that has made its way to these shores) 'comfortable' with the simple, unambiguous 'move'. Using 'transition' as a verb takes us straight into the process and the label by which it is known – the 'transition to democracy'. Bush, whether deliberately or unwittingly, suggests a remote 'process' rather than direct action.

Rubbish

It sometimes works the other way: we turn verbs into nouns. This is a scientist who works for the drugs company Pfizer:

'There is a disconnect in many women between genital changes and mental changes.'

Now why would he want to create a noun where a perfectly good one – 'disconnection' – already exists?

Inevitably, these verb-nouns have become jargon.

Construction companies routinely talk about 'new build'. Sometimes these new words work well. I like 'rubbish' as a verb. It has a powerful ring to it, unlike another voguish alternative, 'diss', as in 'He dissed his opponent.' That has yet to make it into the dictionaries but these things change rapidly.

Sometimes they can be fun. I heard this the other day:

> 'OK, I can see you're not following me. Let's flip-chart it.'

In the context of a business conference, that seemed perfectly natural. At least it woke me up. You often get switches in each direction in the same sentence. This is the economist, Roger Bootle, writing in the *Sunday Telegraph*:

> If the economy continues to grow in the way the Chancellor forecasts, and if the tax take rises the way he says it will, then borrowing will gently trend downwards.

The verb 'take' has now more or less replaced the noun 'revenue', which seems fair enough: it's not as if most of us give the money to the Chancellor voluntarily. I'm less sure about using the noun 'trend' as a verb, but I can't get too upset about it.

I am less happy with the loss of the reflexive pronoun. We seldom commit *ourselves* to something now: we merely commit to it. It is another example of the 'depersonalising' process. The abandonment of certain prepositions is regrettable too. Properly used, they act almost as a lubricant, easing the friction in a sentence. Remove them and the sentence jars:

> The American force battles the insurgents as . . .

No, they don't, they battle against them. Better still, they fight them. 'Battle' is a noun. After the death of Caron Keating a newspaper wrote that:

> Keating's friend, Anthea Turner . . . said she had battled her illness with great courage.

Something else that last sentence might have done was use 'bravely' instead of 'with great courage' but the little suffix '-ly' is going through difficult times. Adverbs are having to fight for their existence. Simon Jenkins, one of our finest columnists, once told me he does not use adverbs in his columns because the verb should speak for itself. That is often the case, but Simon goes too far: sometimes they are essential. Sadly (a lovely, modest little word) we have begun to turn adverbs into adjectives in pointless and tedious phrases. Instead of doing something daily we do it 'on a daily basis'.

CHAPTER SEVEN

Junk Language

I started the last chapter with Barry Humphries and the ghastly Dame Edna. So let's raise the tone with a snappy little quote from the fifteenth-century Franciscan theologian, William of Ockham: '*Entia non sunt multiplicanda praeter necessitatem.*'

If the name is vaguely familiar it's because he is the man who gave us the 'Ockham's razor' approach: 'Entities should not be multiplied beyond necessity.' Or, if you prefer, you should always slice away the clutter in an argument. He was talking about philosophy but it will do very nicely for language. We should not use more words than are necessary. When we do, we should take Ockham's razor to the offending flab. There is plenty of it about. Our language is showing signs of obesity, the consequence of our feeding on junk words.

Tautology is the linguistic equivalent of having chips with rice:

future prospects
past history
past record
future plans
live survivors
safe havens

We talk of 'temper tantrums' and 'new initiatives' (though I concede that in the case of politicians, the 'new' does distinguish from the old ones they recycle). We say 'from whence' and 'he is currently the chairman'. Why 'currently'? What does 'is' mean if not 'currently'? I am constantly invited to read news headlines reporting that 'the planned talks have been cancelled'. How could they be cancelled if they had not been 'planned'? One of the BBC's objectives for 2005 is to 'enhance further the impact' of its global news services. I know how you enhance; I'm damned if I know how you 'enhance further'.

You see signs along the road informing you of 'delays due to an earlier accident', as though they could be due to a later one. Traffic warnings on the radio tell you that road works are 'still continuing', probably adding that they do so 'at this moment in time', as though a moment could be in anything else.

Then there's this sort of thing:

The two brothers both shared the same taste in music.

They could hardly share a different taste, could they? We pad out verbs, 'giving recognition to' something or other, rather than just recognising them. Even the simplest phrases get bloated. We say 'these ones' or even 'these ones here' when all we mean is 'these'. We run away from simple adjectives and take shelter in a rickety noun phrase. We don't say 'the car's colour was dark', but 'the car's colour was a dark one'. We trade in good simple words such as 'once' and 'twice' in favour of the new, improved 'one time' and 'two times'.

None of this matters too much when we are arguing in the pub. Ordinary speech is full of padding. It buys us time while we think. We all do it – except Enoch Powell, of course. Ordinary mortals fill their chatter with ums and ahs and 'I must say' and 'in a sense' and tic words such as 'frankly' and 'honestly' and 'you know' and all the rest (indeed 'and all the rest'). If we didn't, conversation would take on a rather chilling formality.

No, this is about the written word and the language of my own trade, broadcasting. We do not need time to think. We should have thought already – before we wrote it down or sat in front of the microphone. When John Arlott was asked for the secret of his magical cricket commentary, he said that even though he was speaking live he always worked out exactly how his sentence would end before he started it. That, of course, is the counsel of perfection.

Whither Weather?

Broadcasters – especially cricket commentators – talk a lot about the weather. So do we all. I shall have something to say about weather forecasts later on. But just think about the word itself for a moment. It is a wonderful word. It means something both tangible and intangible at the same time, yet we all know exactly where we stand with it. It is a very old Teutonic word, *wedrom*, probably of Indo-European root: **we-* to blow + suffix *-dhro-* or *-tro-*. The compactness of its meaning lends its force to poetry, as here in *The Merchant of Venice:*

> Like the martlet,
> Builds in the weather on the outward wall,
> Even in the force and road of casualty.

It has provided a metaphor for politics. Lloyd George said of his political opponent, Joseph Chamberlain, that 'he makes the political weather'. We know exactly what that means.

But what are we doing with this simple but magnificent word today? We are devaluing it. We seldom get weather any longer. We have 'weather conditions'. This great cosmic word is now shackled in a press-gang with low-life, unambitious words such as 'parking' and 'driving'. They may very well need to be chained to 'conditions' for any sense to be made of them, but the weather *is* the condition. We don't need that tedious add-on word. 'Weather' says it all.

One of the glories of the word is the sense it gives of an agent out of our control, a savage foe or a comforting friend depending on its whim. It needs treating with respect – even reverence.

Alastair Cooke was a master of the English language and, I think, disliked 'weather conditions' as much as I do. He also had a thing about 'area'. He hated it being tacked on when it was not needed. Why say 'the New York area' when you mean New York? He proved his point by amending one of the most famous of all romantic songs: 'Stars fell on the Alabama area'. Quite loses its romance, doesn't it?

But I must bring you back from the heavens to the more mundane scandal of preposition abuse.

Wanna Meet Up?

Some of the obesity of our language comes from our habit of sprinkling prepositions where they should not be. We attach them to verbs that are self-sufficient. We 'test out', 'raise up', 'descend down', 'revert back', 'separate out', 'free up', 'enter in', 'divide up', 'exit out' and 'feed into'. It is not only estate agents who insist that a house 'comprises of' three bedrooms and a through lounge/diner. We write 'all of' when we need no more than 'all' and we even double up prepositions to be on the safe side. Things are 'opposite to' (which compounds the felony), 'up against', 'off of' and 'up until'.

This, inevitably, takes us to 'met up with'. I once wrote a foreword for a book in which I promised a bottle of bubbly to anyone who could provide a justification for this flatulent phrase. I am ashamed to say that I reneged on the deal: it was that or bankruptcy.

It is possible – just possible – that 'met up with' implies something prearranged, whereas 'met' can mean either a prearranged meeting or one that happens by chance. My daughter swears that she would ask a friend to 'meet up' for a drink but if she happened to bump into, say, the Queen in the pub she would say she had 'met' Her Majesty. It is not so long ago that this profoundly irritating usage was restricted to young people, but where did it come from in the first place?

I was offered an intriguing hypothesis by a Polish correspondent, Mr J. L. Klarkowski. The Polish word for 'met' is *spotkałem*, when one is meeting in a casual manner. But the phrase to use for meeting in an intentional manner is *spotkałem się z*, which literally means 'met oneself with'. The suggestion is that the enormous Polish-speaking population in the United States has transferred this usage into American English, and now it has arrived here.

I've no idea if this is true, but no one has come up with a better explanation. Even if it is true, I am offering only a partial concession. I am not convinced that the fat version is used only for the specific meaning of an intentional meeting. And I *am* convinced that before long 'meet up with' will be the standard bloated phrase for every sort of meeting, intentional or otherwise. That's because obesity breeds laziness and sloppiness. As for me, I shall go to my grave saying 'met', entirely confident in the knowledge that no one will ever be confused as to what I mean. We managed without 'up with' for quite a long time and we can still manage without it.

Let's Terminate

Perhaps one of the reasons we slide around with all these prepositions is that we do not trust ourselves to use the right one. We keep dumping one for another. So we get 'different to' instead of 'different from', and 'bored of' instead of 'bored with'. Guards on trains have started to say 'We shall shortly be arriving into King's Cross.' What is wrong with 'at'? The same people tell us that once it has arrived 'into' King's Cross, the train will 'terminate', which is a pretty scary thought. Perhaps they just want to make sure all the passengers (sorry, customers) get off quickly – as if they're not late enough already.

More likely, though, this is a textbook case of language inflation. A station can no longer be simply a station. It must be called (under the influence of American English and to the intense annoyance of many) a 'train station'.

Some prepositions are becoming quite predatory. They try to take over the grazing pasture of their unsuspecting cousins. John Radford, a professor of psychology at the University of East London, wrote a witty article in the journal of the Queen's English Society, called 'On "on"'. He proved that 'on' is a most aggressive little word.

Its colonising ambitions involve supplanting

in: 'on Regent Street' or 'on a football team';
beside: the house is 'on the river';
to: we have 'one-on-one' relationships;
against: there is 'black-on-black' violence;
for: the 'committee on standards in public life';
with: 'on a mushroom sauce';
at: 'on the weekend';
of: 'a grasp on British history'.

That's eight to be going on with. You will spot more for yourself.

It's great fun but it can be risky, this business of spotting solecisms. I played the smart-arse with a friend who said 'oblivious of'. Doesn't everyone know it is meant to be 'oblivious to'? Er, no, actually. I appealed to Fowler's *Modern English Usage* and the great man let me down. It seems the meaning of 'oblivious' has shifted a little. Originally it meant 'forgetful, unmindful' and was followed by 'of'. But it came also to mean 'unaware of, unconscious of', and in this usage either 'to' or 'of' was deployed. The *OED* of 1904 frowned on this, but R. W. Burchfield, Fowler's most recent editor, was more tolerant. It seems that usage now authorises both.

Take Issue With That

I found that mildly upsetting. I have *always* said 'oblivious to' and felt rather smug about it. You may be thinking, 'Poor chap, he should get a life.' You have a point. What has changed, now that I know it's okay to say 'oblivious of'? Nothing. All I have shown – for the umpteenth time – is that usage changes. All Fowler can do is describe the changes. If the changes have become acceptable, that is the only justification needed. So maybe I should stop fussing about prepositions and language obesity and all the rest of it. Maybe I should chill out, as my children would put it. Or, rather, 'chill': the preposition was dropped long ago.

Well, maybe, but I think there is more going on here. It is not just the usual evolution of usage: it is of a particular sort. And it can be exposed by yet another little shift in the way we use prepositions. In this case, it is John Radford's aggressive 'on' that is the loser. The winner is the preposition 'around'. People speak these days of things being centred 'around' something, not 'on' it. That is both ungrammatical and revealing. To be centred or focused 'on' something implies a clear and precise target. A bullseye is scored. But to be centred 'around' something means the darts may not even hit the board. We're flailing around, throwing our darts broadly in its direction. We are succumbing to imprecision.

You can see this in another cause to which 'around' has attached itself: 'issues around'. We would once have said,

There is a problem with class.

Later, if we wanted to be a little more tentative or if we were politicians who were scared of any possible repercussions:

There is an issue about class.

Now you hear:

There are issues around class.

There is a double evasiveness going on here.

'Issues around' seems to take us half-way to nothing being said at all. It puts me in mind of Alan Bennett's father, who once said to the young Alan of his aunt: 'She's a marathon talker, Alan, is your aunt. But you're no further on when she's finished.' I also think of the people who bought houses on a new development in Weston-super-Mare in 2003. They expected the odd little problem – anyone who has bought a new home does – but this was a nightmare. Floors were uneven; roof tiles were fitted wrongly and so were the windows; oven wiring was dangerous; central heating had to be re-installed. The list was extraordinary. In one case the entire front of a house had to be removed because the brickwork was so shoddy.

When the builders finally got round to apologising this was how they put it:

> We were aware of the build quality issues on one home but we were not aware that the problem may extend to other properties.

Here's a company building houses that make the buyers' lives a misery and they can't bring themselves to use that admirable word 'problems'. Instead there are 'build quality issues'. Maybe we need another word for 'apology'.

Euphemistically Speaking

The motivation for euphemism is usually pretty clear. You can see why 'slaughterhouse' gave way to 'abattoir'. The sound of the French word has none of the savagery of 'slaughter', with its reminder of what happened to the sweet little lamb that has ended up as chops on the butcher's shelf.

I guarantee that 'butcher' will be the next to go.

No doubt when all our local butchers have been driven out of business – which can't be long now – the marauding supermarkets will find a cosier word for their rows of chill cabinets masquerading as a butcher's shop. Just as some children today have no idea what connects a carton of milk to a cow, children in future will never see blood dripping from a butchered joint on a slab and they will be encouraged to think that all meat comes naturally wrapped in Cellophane. Did I say 'meat'? Try 'protein packs'.

You can also see why 'abortion' has almost given way to 'termination'. You 'terminate a pregnancy', which is a state or a condition. You abort a foetus – which is a human being.

Bernard Levin believed that all euphemisms are lies. He admired the writer Marghanita Laski, who translated 'simple, inexpensive gowns for the fuller figure' into 'nasty, cheap dresses for fat old women'.

They are used for a particular purpose and that purpose is to change reality. When British Rail announced in the eighties that it was abolishing second class travel, Levin pointed out that it was doing no such thing. It was just calling it something else: standard class. First class remained – and you can't have a first without there being a second.

I spoke to a man from Scottish and Southern Energy about what his company was doing to the countryside and he resolutely refused to use the word 'pylon'. Instead, he banged on about 'electrical transmission infrastructure'. You can hear the PR consultant briefing him: 'On no account use the word "pylon", Alan. It's got baggage. It's got resonance. It's got negative feedback. Stick with the technical phrase and people won't be reminded of the problem we're trying to get them to forget. Just keep talking about issues around electrical transmission infrastructure".' Not that he would have used the word 'problem' either. It would probably have been 'challenges'.

Here's a magnificent euphemism, coined by a businessman who was making a case for an ambitious project for which he was trying to raise a lot of money. He admitted exaggerating its potential earning power. When, some years later, he was tackled about it, he was asked if he'd been dishonest. 'No,' he said, 'I was telling future truths.' I leave it to you to judge whether he was, in the euphemistic language of another of my interviewees, 'ethically challenged'.

Euphemism has, I suppose, always been with us. Not all of it is to be derided. The great John Mortimer remembers being phoned by Jessica Mitford, who had just been told she was terminally ill. 'Bit of a bloody nuisance,' she said, 'I've only got three months to live.' Euphemism can be moving.

Out with What?

But what seems different today is the number of new words and phrases that add nothing to the language and simply sound pretentious: words such as 'infotainment' and 'infomediary'; phrases such as 'paradigm shift' and 'step-change'. 'Outwith' has become fashionable. One of our political correspondents at the BBC insists on using it, as in:

> 'One senses that outwith Downing Street there are very few senior political figures who now believe John Scarlett should take up his post as head of MI6.'

I suppose he meant 'outside' Downing Street. So why didn't he say so? There is a spate of '-ee' words too. They once had some sort of purpose, either borrowed from the French feminine (fiancée) or distinguishing a relationship (employer/employee). Now they are springing up without any of that justification. People who escape from prison are 'escapees', rather than escapers. People who share flats are 'co-habitees' and not cohabitants. And then there are 'standees', who can't find a seat on the bus. Does that make those who can 'sittees'?

For years we have had 'grandees', who tend not to use buses – although I recall fondly the way lesser members of the Royal Family and minor crowned heads of Europe were bundled into a coach at the Golden Jubilee a few years ago and whisked off to St Paul's Cathedral, for all the world as if they were a group of OAPs on a day's outing. I imagined them getting there and being told, 'You've got two hours for the ceremony. There are no public lavatories in the cathedral. And I want you all back here at two thirty sharp or the bus leaves without you!'

I suspect they might have had issues around that.

CHAPTER EIGHT

Damn Yankees?

If you wanted to study the influence of America on the way we speak, you could read a thousand learned essays on the subject. Or you could pour yourself a glass of wine, draw your chair up to the fire and watch a couple of re-runs of *Friends*. It was the world's most popular television sitcom – every one of its 236 episodes watched by hundreds of millions of people around the world – and it created its own language. All successful programmes implant catchphrases in our consciousness. For a decade it was impossible to say, 'Nice to see you,' without someone adding, 'To see you . . . nice.' Like irritating advertising jingles heard a thousand times, they never quite leave us. I can still remember, 'Can I do you now, sir?' on the Home Service of BBC wireless more than fifty years ago. But they were meant to make us laugh. If we repeated them we did so to amuse. With *Friends* it is different.

I'm not suggesting for a moment that the Americanisation of our language is new. Even before the first GI landed on these shores with packets of nylon stockings, we were imitating American English. Some of the vocabulary has been with us so long we have forgotten where it came from: 'baby-sitter' and 'blurb'; 'editorial' and 'anyway'. We would have no 'commuters' without the Americans, nor could we 'reckon' their numbers.

In the past few years there has been some traffic the other way. Professor Ben Yagoda of Delaware University has found that 'Briticisms' are cropping up all over the place these days. Americans have adopted our 'sell-by' date instead of their 'expiration' date and our 'run-up' to elections. They have also, more's the pity, taken to 'gone missing' where they would once have used the grammatical 'disappeared'. That's particularly annoying. I've been trying for years to ban 'gone missing' from the BBC. Now there's no hope.

Noah Webster, whose name has been immortalised through *Webster's Dictionaries*, was wrong when he predicted in 1789 that our two languages would grow apart and eventually become as different as German and Dutch. Instead there has been a cross-pollination – with most of the pollen drifting from west to east.

When *Friends* appeared here, young people began speaking differently. They adopted the syntax and the intonations of the six American friends. 'I'm, like, really sincere about this.' 'Could I *be* any more excited?' 'This is *so* not an exaggeration.' 'So, like, chill.'

But older people do not chill at that sort of thing. Older people (stand by for a sweeping generalisation) do not approve. To judge by my own mail, the Americanisation of our language is one of those things that delivers a nasty jolt. Yet we are not, in general, hostile to the influence of other languages.

Whose Influence?

The Anglo-Saxon language developed here after the sixth century and became remarkably successful in these islands and far beyond. In his book *The Adventure of English*, Melvyn Bragg suggests one of the reasons was its readiness to absorb the influence of other languages. Old Norse, Latin, French and Irish were the most obvious.

You can still see this in the way Indian words gain currency. The *Oxford English Dictionary* already contained many Hindi words from a previous wave of influence – 'bungalow', 'shampoo' and 'thug', for example. Asian 'yoof-speak' is adding more. It now includes 'badmash' (naughty) and 'Angrez' (an English person). In *The Kumars at No. 42* Meera Syal is making sure cool people talk not of 'underwear' but of 'chuddies'.

But the influence of American English breeds a special resentment. Perhaps that is because it exposes one of our more smug illusions. We like to tell ourselves (and, even more, the French) that our language is establishing itself as the common language of the world: the one that everyone chooses to speak. So it is. Yet it is not English that is becoming the world's second language, but American. Our predicament is not so different from what the French are always getting agitated about. There is resentment that our former colony has stolen our crown. We like to think that we are, as Harold Macmillan put it to John F. Kennedy, Greece to their Rome. Naturally, the language is by rights 'ours', so anything they might do to it is bound to be a debasement. Self flattery is seldom justified. American English is anything but a poor or (worse still) vulgar man's British English. There are some grounds for saying it is in much better shape than our version.

Let's Party!

Americans who care about their language tend to care a great deal. William Safire has been writing for the *New York Times* since I was in short trousers. He now has a weekly column on how English is used. In his latest book, *No Uncertain Terms*, he quotes from some correspondence with a certain

Preston A. Britner, assistant professor of family
studies (yes, I know) at the University of Connecticut.
The argument is over the respective merits of 'since'
and 'because', as used in an earlier contribution by
a chap called Zinsser. In academic America lots
of people get worked up about this sort of thing.
Here's a part (a very small part) of what the professor
wrote:

> 'Since' is used in a nontemporal fashion . . . 'be-
> cause' would be the more appropriate word choice.
> It is a bit picky, but it is an excellent example of a
> commonly accepted verbal usage that is technically
> incorrect and seems to be misused more and more
> frequently in the written language in recent years.
> Perhaps the fact that this misuse is common in
> the spoken language would justify Zinsser's misuse
> according to his tenet? I, for one, would prefer to
> protect correct word usage. As many of my students
> could affirm, I never let it slide when grading
> papers . . .

It was that last bit that caught my attention. I
thought of my friend, the timorous professor, and
his trepidation at making any criticism of his
students' command of English lest he be accused of
'discrimination'. There are no such inhibitions in
the States: professors just go for it.

American English has held on to various forms of usage that we have jettisoned without any good reason. 'Gotten' is the most obvious. But there is another that crops up and never fails to irritate:

'Let's go party!'

It is more than the turning of the noun into a verb that annoys people: it's the dropping of the 'and'. Yet that was how we commonly spoke until the seventeenth century, according to Fowler, who cites *The Winter's Tale*:

I'll go see if the bear be gone.

Abraham Lincoln, in his famous magnanimous gesture after victory in the civil war, instructed his staff:

'Go bid the band play "Dixie"!'

He could have said,

'Go and bid the band play "Dixie"!'

but it just doesn't have the same energy.

May I Be Your Cuddle Monkey?

Then there is the sheer inventiveness with language that comes from America. The television programme *Buffy the Vampire Slayer* has bred its own published lexicon, *Slayer Slang*, with such phrases as 'pointy' (the opposite of pointless), 'cuddle monkey' (your male lover), 'carbon dated' (which might accurately describe most of my clothes), and this one:

> 'Don't invade her personal space or she'll go all, like, special forces on you.'

Isn't it magnificent? You don't have to speak this extraordinary language to know exactly what it means. Sir Howard Davies, the director of the London School of Economics, picked that one out as his favourite when he reviewed the book. I imagine him using it when he's warning a professor about a particularly volatile colleague. Maybe the head of the Gender Institute.

Still, there is plenty to moan about and that's partly because we cannot escape it. You may avoid *Friends Speak* or *Slayer Slang* by refusing to talk to anyone under the age of, say, fifty who watches television, but the only way to avoid computer-speak is to dump your computer. Once you have one, that is not an option. They take you over, like those sinister aliens that come out of pods and bundle you into garbage trucks – or dustcarts, as we once said. The technology is theirs, so the language is theirs. Once you have booted up and logged on (why not logged in?) you are theirs for life. If you have a problem (*when* you have a problem) you must do your best to communicate with the Lords of the Universe, known more prosaically as the 'help desk'. This cannot be done.

Communication suggests an exchange. There is no exchange. You try, from the depths of your profound ignorance, to tell them what the problem is and they tell you what to do about it. It is a little like asking where you can get a cup of tea in one of the remoter villages in China. They want to help very much indeed but they speak a different language. You are pathetically grateful for everything they tell you even though you know your chances of actually doing it and solving the problem are roughly nil.

Add to this that American domination of computer-speak forces us to change our spelling (program, disk) and that this spelling imperialism now stretches via your desk-top through spellcheck and beyond and you end up with a deep sense of grievance at what the Americans are doing to us.

Computer speech is perforce a part of our common language. We'll just have to bloody well learn it if we are to survive and retain our sanity. It's not as if we haven't learned plenty of other American English.

Friends Corrupt

The French moan about Americanisms creeping into their language. Our problem is different because we share the same language – up to a point. It is easier to corrupt English English than it is to corrupt French French. Is corrupt too strong a word? Not when 'transport' becomes 'transportation' and 'rain' becomes 'precipitation', it isn't. And there are many more (or 'plenty more' to use the American variation) where they came from. It is also their fault that we say 'in light of events' and 'the problem is is'. Why, why have we adopted that silly one?

Unlike *Friends Speak* this sort of thing is not restricted to youngsters. I have a boss who is so clever he uses words like 'ratiocination' when you're chatting in the pub and even seems to know what they mean. When he speaks you can hear not only the commas and full stops, but you see the colons and semi-colons hanging in the air. To call him articulate is to call Goya fairly good with a brush. And yet the other day he said, 'First of all . . . and second of all,' without even a slight blush of shame. I thought it might have been irony (I said he was clever) but he did it again and clearly meant it. Why not 'third of all and fourth of all' into infinity? 'Already' is taking off here too, as in 'I saw it already' – Yiddish via American into English. Go figure.

Some American constructions can be alarming for the literally minded. When an American pilot tells you he will be taking off 'momentarily' he does not mean the take-off will be followed swiftly by a crash landing. Hopefully not. And that's another one for which we have the Americans to blame – probably German Americans. '*Hoffentlich*' is used in German to start a sentence with the meaning 'I hope'. Convert it into 'hopefully' and a whole era of verbal misuse is born.

Why, since we do not play 'ball games', do we have 'ballparks' everywhere? I can live, just about, with 'firefighters' because there is no reason why a woman should be called a 'fireman', but 'firefight' has become ubiquitous and it is annoying. So is 'Prime Minister Blair'. We do not have such a figure. 'Prime Minister' is an office, not a title – which, of course, might be held by Mr Brown or even somebody else by the time you read this.

You may think this is all petty stuff. It may not even make you mad (remember when we would have said angry?) so, hey, as we must say now, let's get real. Let's think about the next generation.

So I'm Like . . .

My older children spoke fluent American – with perfect American accents – when they were young. That's hardly surprising since we lived in America for nearly six years. They lost nearly all of it when we moved to South Africa. My four-year-old son has yet to cross the Atlantic but he uses, 'Hey!' routinely and calls his pushchair a 'buggy' and biscuits 'cookies'. I am waiting – with some trepidation – for the first 'Omigod!'

What else will he 'say'? Probably nothing. On the basis of the available evidence, the verb may no longer exist. It was already under threat from our own usage:

'So I went, "You didn't!" and he went, "I did!"'

There is a rococo variation on this. Sometimes the speaker not only goes, but revolves: 'So I turned round and I went, "Well that's it then,' and he turned round and he went . . .' That is no longer cool.

Now it has become

'So I'm like "You didn't!" and he's like "I did!"'

The verb 'say' or even 'go' has gone. The next to

go is tenses. Who needs the past tense when history no longer exists and nor does the future when no one is giving it any thought? Let's just bundle everything into the present. That seems to be what children are doing increasingly – and not just American children. Ian Jack, the editor of the magazine *Granta*, has written about his eleven-year-old daughter who speaks only in the present tense:

> 'We're on the *train?* and Tom's Give me my mobile back and she's like No go away and he's like No please Rache I really need it when this *man?* comes up and he's looking for a *seat?* and Rache throws the phone at Tom and it *hits?* this man and he's like angry and the train is coming into Potters *Bar?* and . . .'

You have heard it for yourself, of course. But they are children and, as I have already acknowledged, there is no reason why children should not have their own language. They always have and they always will. It is a part of growing up. But much of this stuff is spreading into what I have called the common language. Academics are among the worst culprits. I don't care what they do in their colleges but it is profoundly irritating on programmes such as Melvyn Bragg's *In Our Time*. They talk of historical events as though they are happening as they speak, rather than a few centuries ago: 'Henry VIII dissolves the monasteries because he wants . . .'

It has become almost obligatory for Sunday newspapers to start their double-page accounts of the big event of the past week with this sort of thing:

> It is Wednesday morning. It is a cold, gloomy day in Washington. President Bush has to decide . . .

Fowler points out that the use of the present tense for past events goes back at least to thirteenth-century English and possibly even to Old English. It is true that it can add dramatic immediacy, but we are now doing it everywhere as though we cannot trust the distance that the past tense lends an account. It is as if no one will believe what we have to say unless we transport them into an imaginary present where they can see it for themselves, so to speak.

There is a similar implicit lack of confidence in the other habit we've picked up from American television. The rising inflection, as Ian Jack notes, was once used only to mark a question. Now it is used to emphasise a statement. Or, rather, emphasise a *statement*?

Again, defenders of American English can easily point out that there have always been verbal devices in British English for doing this sort of thing. Take this passage given by Lady Bell as an example of fashionable speech in 1907 and cited in Jose Harris's book, *Private Lives, Public Spirit: Britain 1870– 1914*:

> 'And then, do you see, I said "no" – sort of very loudly, do you see? And really sort of meaning it, don't you know what I mean? And as for him – well, do you see, he was sort of bothered – you see what I mean, don't you?'

It is both a million miles from, and very close to, the speech of Ian Jack's daughter. 'Do you see?' is the posh 1907 version of the rising inflection. The difference is that we are now leaving it to the Americans to provide us with our linguistic tics as well as with our words and idioms.

This Has Got to Be Bad ...

Here's another American import:

> Therapy's got to be the best thing that ever happened to her.

The 'got to be' construction seems, on the face of it, extremely self-confident – so confident we are almost bullied into conceding that there cannot be another point of view. British English has its own milder version – as in this from the programme for an Arts Council conference held in Manchester in 2004:

> The highlight of the past year must of course be Liverpool's successful 2008 European Capital of Culture bid.

In her *Spectator* column Dot Wordsworth character-ised this use of 'must' as 'epistemic', as distinct from the 'deontic' use: 'you must work harder'. And, no, I had no idea what 'deontic' meant either. The dic-tionary says it is 'of the science of duty and moral obligation'.

The interesting thing about this usage is that it is almost always self-defeating. If we are effectively bullied into accepting something – 'It's got to be . . .' – the temptation is to respond: 'No, it hasn't! Why has it "got" to be? As a matter of fact, I think her therapy was the worst thing that ever happened to her.'

More importantly, the self-confidence is fake: it betrays the speaker's lack of confidence in his con-victions. He seeks shelter in an imagined consensus he invites us to join.

Lack of self-confidence plays other tricks. Here's

Tom Cruise answering a question about whether he might one day marry again:

> 'Yeah, yeah, definitely. I think that I don't have anything like, "I am never going to get married again" . . . I think if that time comes again when I am going to get married, I will do it.'

It is as if two Tom Cruises are involved here: the straightforward, subjective one who 'will do it' – get married – and the other, the distanced, objective one, for whom 'the time [may come] again when I am going to get married'. You can spot the ubiquitous therapy at work here.

I'm Good

Ask almost anyone under thirty, especially those who aspire to being 'cool', how they are. A few years ago they would have said, 'I'm well.' Now they say, 'I'm good.' It may be accompanied by a gentle nod of the head and the attempt at a Tom Cruise smile. It makes you want to cuff them smartly across the back of the head and snap, 'Let me be the judge of that, you smug prat!'

Irritating it may be, but it is grammatically sound. 'Well' and 'good' can both be adjectives. So, technically, it is accurate to say 'good'. But they don't mean the same thing. 'Well' is about health. 'Good' brings with it moral overtones – especially when it is delivered with the infuriating smile. The American song-writer Randy Newman knew what he was doing when he wrote a brilliant satire on the complacency of a certain kind of self-satisfied young American and called it 'My Life Is Good'.

Yet another American idiom that's creeping in combines the distancing and the complacency. You offer someone a drink. Instead of saying, 'No, thank you,' they say,

'I don't do alcohol.'

The smugness hardly needs pointing out, but the way it comes about is interesting. It's the distancing effect again. He implies it was all thoroughly looked into and a policy decision was taken to eschew alcohol. So now the issue is closed. We have 'moved on'. We don't have to address it any more.

The distancing is simultaneously defensive and aggressive. It says, 'I don't want to talk about it, and I don't want to confront anything that might challenge my sense of being "good".' I heard it when I passed a man collecting money for charity in the street. As he cheerily rattled his tin at a woman passing by, she simply said, 'I don't do charity.' And the man with the tin just smiled at her.

Bring It On!

Will we all end up speaking American English one day? Quite possibly. 'Trucks' clog our roads. We watch 'movies'. Our youngsters sound as if they were brought up in Greenwich Village or LA. 'Gotten' has even begun to return. And yet, for all the garbage (or do I mean trash?), there are some things to be said for the language.

In American politics and public life generally there is often a directness that I would love to hear on *Today*. We can only admire the presidential candidate who, when he learned he had been defeated, declared with great dignity, 'The American people have spoken . . .' a slight pause and then '. . . the bastards.'

And let us also salute Colonel John Coleman, the chief of staff of the 1st Marine Expeditionary Force. He was talking to journalists in April 2004 during the stand-off between American forces and Iraqi insurgents at Fallujah. You have to imagine him speaking with all the vigour and fast-talking genial enthusiasm of a character in *South Park*:

> The tactical action is never in doubt. I will win this fight. I will bust his back. And he will be dead. OK? There's no doubt about it. Will it be a little more bloody cos he has a chance to reinforce?

Maybe. Maybe I'll just get a little more creative about how I shoot him. You know, when it comes down to throwing lead, we have some techniques that are masterful, and we will use every one of them . . . We'll win that fight. There's no doubt in my mind about that. But the result of that fight and the way it's carried out will have an impact far beyond the value of who I just shot. Especially if it's the wrong guys. Especially if there's, God forbid, some civilians in the way of my line of fire, or the collateral damage which I try my best to control. But, you know, when you throw things down that explode in the manner they do, things happen.

Indeed they do.

Stop Press

You know how twitchers get terribly excited when someone reports the first sighting of a foreign bird on British soil? They all rush off to the furthest corner of the land to watch the lesser-spotted Siberian sparrow perched gloomily on a branch, baffled by the sight of all those people wearing anoraks and powerful binoculars round their necks and wondering how the hell it's going to get home. Well, I've done it – not with a bird, but a word that has migrated from North America and landed here. I think I may be the first person to have spotted 'diaper' in normal usage. It appeared in the *Daily Mail* on Saturday, 4 August, in a story about potty training. Is this the beginning of the end for 'nappy'?

American English is now used routinely on packaging by fast-food retailers who want to appeal to young people. I have come across one written almost entirely in American. Golden Wonder produce a truly disgusting snack (sorry, 'snak') called Nik Naks. The flavour (flavor) I tried was 'rib 'n' saucy' – 'and' disappeared quite a long time ago – and the pack carries the mandatory ingredients list. It calls it 'What's in 'em?'. Naturally the company would like to know what you think of their product. Here is how they phrase the invitation:

If you wanna give us any feedback on your Nik Naks experience, email us . . .

Finally, there is some public-spirited advice on the package: 'Bin yer bag.' They do not stipulate whether you should eat the contents first.

CHAPTER NINE

Words Without Thought

It's a funny thing about clichés. We simultaneously love and hate them. We use them all the time and we get sniffy when other people do the same. Every so often the Plain English Campaign publishes a list and for the next few days you cannot pick up a paper without seeing them all lovingly quoted. Reporters are ordered to ring up famous people and ask them for their most hated cliché. Competitions are held to see who can construct a sentence containing the most and the worst. Public figures such as Tony Benn – normally concerned only with the deeply serious ishoos – join in the fun. It seems to have become a new national pastime.

No doubt there will be a television series one day: *Name That Cliché*. Football managers and 'HR' executives will be forbidden to take part – for the same reason that we ban professionals from choosing their area of expertise for *Mastermind*. It just wouldn't be fair to the others. Spin-offs will include the *Great Book of British Clichés* and T-shirts bearing the worst. Award ceremonies will be held to honour those who create new clichés. There would be much agreeable argument over how long a given phrase would have to survive to qualify for entry. Is it too early, for instance, to honour 'moving the goalposts' or 'drawing a line in the sand' or 'naming and shaming' or 'blue-sky thinking'?

'Road map' is a new kid on the block, which is itself a qualifier. These are all still wet behind the ears compared with, well, 'wet behind the ears' or 'raining cats and dogs', which is so old it has disappeared. But most live on. We trot them out endlessly (rather than avoid them like the plague – which must be even older) and we get very angry about them. This is odd, especially given that they must have become clichés in the first place because we liked them. It is also heartening. It could be that we are merely showing off when we make a fuss about clichés (aren't we smart to spot them?) but it could equally be that we value our language and do not like to see it diminished. We recognise that endless repetition of a cliché flogs its original meaning to death.

Want Your Thinking Done for You?

Julia Cresswell compiled the *Penguin Dictionary of Clichés* and wrote in the introduction that a cliché is something that 'does your thinking for you'. She's right. If we use words without a direct link to our own thought what we end up with is mere words – just noise – rather than the communication of one mind with another.

Cliché has a younger sibling: jargon. With jargon the process is slightly different, although the effect is the same. Living meaning becomes petrified. Within any piece of jargon there is usually buried an original thought, but the outer shell of the phrase has become so hard that it can no longer be penetrated.

Here is a relatively new one I came across in a letter written by Lord Penrose, the man sent off to look into the Equitable Life scandal, to the House of Commons Treasury Committee.

> Let me start with the timetable going forward and my own commitment to achieving it . . . We are actually aiming to complete the report, including maxwellisation, in June.

Let us wearily put aside the notion of timetables going forward – as against going backwards presumably – and consider 'maxwellisation'.

You may remember that Robert Maxwell was the newspaper proprietor who stole his employees' pensions, so you may think you can work out what it means. You will almost certainly be wrong. Its very formation is an outrage: a proper noun (Maxwell) extended into a verb (maxwellise), extended again into another noun. Apparently 'maxwellisation' is a term used about official investigative reports to mean that organisations and individuals fingered in them have the right to comment on them before they are published. All clear now? Maxwell himself would have been proud of it – as obscure and ugly as his accounting methods.

Mantra Gurus

The worst jargon is dreamed up by management gurus, some of whom make fortunes telling managers how to run their businesses. Since they have mostly never run a business of their own they must conceal this by using language that holds no meaning but creates an illusion. The illusion is that this meaningless language is actually profound. It is vital that you speak it. If you cannot you will appear a fool to those who can.

So they teach their willing victims what their absurd words mean – or, rather, what they say they mean. Then, when the clients have mastered the code, the gurus create a new theory. Obviously this requires that the clients must learn a new language so that they can follow the new theory. Thus they perpetuate themselves. They are very clever people, these gurus. Often wrong – but very clever. They cast a long shadow over our language.

Michael Shea spent years working for the Queen as her press secretary. Then he left the Palace to work for an international PLC. I had lunch with him shortly afterwards and asked how he liked the new job. 'It's terrible,' he groaned. 'I sit there in the board room and half the time I've no idea what they're talking about.' I was puzzled: Shea is a very bright man indeed. I met him again a few months later and asked him the same question. He beamed. 'It's great! I've learned the language.'

But how can anyone bear it? Lucy Kellaway is a *Financial Times* journalist who spent many hours heroically reading the chairmen's letters in a batch of annual reports from British companies. Almost all of them parroted a version of this:

We remain focused on leveraging the strong positions and relationships we enjoy in key markets . . . Looking forward we have taken clear steps to remove impediments to future progress.

That little masterpiece came from the chairman of BAe Systems, Sir Richard Evans. Even without the jargon it is execrable. '*Future* progress', eh? No doubt they also learned valuable lessons (lessons are always valuable, never deeply embarrassing) from 'past history'. Does it tell you anything? Of course not. It can be instructive in these cases to insert the little word 'not' to appreciate how vacuous this stuff is. Thus:

> We do *not* remain focused. We have *not* taken clear steps [whatever a 'clear' step may be]. We are *not* going to remove impediments.

They're hardly likely to say any of that, are they? Incidentally, it works even better with politicians: 'We pledge *not* to reduce poverty . . . *not* to ensure that every child gets a first-class education . . . *not* to ensure a fair and just society . . . *not* to be tough on crime.' Try it for yourself some time.

Often the language is used with so little regard for what it means that it achieves the opposite of what was intended. This sort of thing is common:

> We must innovate to survive. Failure is not an option.

A senior manager in one of Britain's largest companies was at a meeting where those banal words were delivered from the lectern. He wrote to tell me what effect they had on him and his colleagues:

> You can imagine just how many people were prompted to innovate; to attempt the untried, in the light of the second imperative. Change, that all-encompassing word, has become a universal corporate mantra. We must change to survive. But change from what and to what? Change for change's sake is no solution to anything. Most people actually eschew change. It is emotionally disruptive, stress inducing and threatens that most fundamental of human needs – stability.

He left the meeting not only demoralised but puzzled at the failure of the people running this vast organisation to recognise the effect their words were having on the staff.

Bottom Line

Is there any thinking at all behind this dreary, off-the-peg, meaningless language or is it simply intended to conceal any thought that there might be? Professor John Kay, a student of the business world, thinks it is a bit of both. The stock phrases bandied about are symptoms of laziness and a failure to think clearly but also 'they are used in business *because* they are vague'. People who run businesses are held to account by their shareholders and employees so they usually try to say as little as possible. Cliché and jargon provide camouflage.

Don Watson says in his book, *Death Sentence: the Decay of Public Language*, that when businessmen use language they 'do not exactly speak or write, so much as *implement* it'.

The problem is that it's catching. It was businessmen who came up with such hideous expressions as '24/7' and 'bottom line' (increasingly used without the definite article). Now we're all doing it – or nearly all of us. We have 'negative' feelings and 'positive' emotions these days. This language is so limited.

Business-speak is probably inevitable in the board room or the annual report – although, even there, it would make sense to use a language the share-holders can understand – but executives also do it when they move into the outside world. This is Lloyd Dorfman, the chairman and chief executive of the foreign-exchange company Travelex, announcing a deal in which his company agreed to sponsor Covent Garden and the National Theatre so that they could sell some of their seats for a tenner:

We are a global business and we regard ourselves as world-leading and world-beating [aren't they the same?]. The great thing about this is that it is not just badging a season – we are really engaging with both institutions to provide a to-die-for, incredible deal for the consumer. It is much more pro-active [ugh] than just sticking your name above a production.

You know what he means. You can even detect a genuine bit of real enthusiasm struggling to escape, but the leaden clichés of business-speak drag him down and in the end he drowns. A pity.

Bingo!

I have a friend who is based in Europe and works for an American company. A lot of his time – far too much, he says – is spent on conference calls with head office. It's not so much that he doesn't understand the jargon. His problem is that he hates it. He confided in one of his colleagues, who told him hating it was not allowed. Then this arrived by email:

Bingo

Do you keep falling asleep in meetings and seminars? What about those long and boring conference calls? Here is the way to change all that!

How to play: Check off each block when you hear these words during a meeting, seminar, or phone call. When you get five blocks horizontally, vertically, or diagonally, stand up and shout **Bullshit!!**

Synergy	Strategic Fit	Gap Analysis	Best Practice	Bottom Line
Revisit	Bandwidth	Hardball	Out of the Loop	Bench-mark
Value-Added	Proactive	Win-Win	Mindset	Fast Track
Touch Base	Empower	Knowledge Base	Total Quality	Result-Driven
Think Outside the Box	Ball Park	Game Plan	Client-Focused	Leverage

Attached to the email were testimonials from satis-fied players:

'I had only been in the meeting for five minutes when I won.' Bob W

'My attention span at meetings has improved dra-matically.' David D

'What a gas. Meetings will never be the same for me after my first win.' Bill R

'The atmosphere was tense in the last process meet-ing as 14 of us waited for the 5th box.' Ben G

'The speaker was stunned as eight of us screamed "Bullshit" for the third time in 2 hours.' Kathleen L

This sort of thing is catching on. I met another businessman who plays a variation of the game in his company. In this one you have to identify the most outrageous phrase. He won with 'retro-aspirationalist'. A worthy victor. A BBC boss told me about having to decide where staff fit into the 'sanction/reward matrix'. It means whether they should be sacked or given a pay rise. That, in turn, might depend on whether they are 'progressing the latest initiative' or even being responsible for 'creative icebergs'. If not, they may be 'de-individuated', which cannot possibly be as painful as it sounds. Deloitte Consulting has produced a piece of software called 'Bull Fighter' that you can install in your computer to detect jargon and give you a score. It is supposed to 'take the bull by the horns and stamp out business jargon'. But it's probably too late. The virus has spread way beyond the board room and the business meeting.

Healthy Talk

Remember this from the first chapter?

> Each Specialist Library will be the product of a community of practice of all those interested in knowledge mobilisation and localisation in their domain.

That is how people in the National Health Service now communicate with each other. It is part of an advertisement published by the NHS Information Authority seeking tenders to set up specialist libraries in the new national electronic library for health. I think what it means is that if you want the job you need to be interested in it. But I'm not sure. This one is a little easier. The job in question is 'Manual hygiene trainer'. The successful applicant will offer 'hands-on' advice to health workers with 'particular attention to cross-infection minimisation'. Could it mean 'teach them how to wash their hands'?

The great skill of management-speak is its ability to state the obvious in such a way that normal human beings won't have a clue what it means. My own theory is that it's the lawyer syndrome: if we knew what they were talking about we wouldn't need them.

I challenge you to read the following extract from the *Health Service Journal* on something called 'change management' – itself a misnomer because all management is about dealing with change. If everything always stayed the same why would you need managers? It was written by a Dr Jay Bevington who is – and I swear I am not making this up – 'the associate director of the NHS clinical governance support team's performance development team'. I wonder how many nurses you could pay with the money that that little lot costs. Anyway, here is what the good Dr Bevington wrote:

Principle 4: focus on and nurture the foundations of cultural health

Performance is the result of the day-to-day choices and actions taken by individuals at all levels. For example, trusts in which people take risks, are creative and innovative and use their initiative are likely to be three-star organisations (Mannion *et al*, 2003).

Similarly, Ghoshal and Bartlett (1997) found that an organisation's ability to continually improve and renew itself depended on these behaviours [*sic*] at a local level:

- execution/delivery of healthcare promises;
- collaboration/dialogue;
- commitment to, and engagement with, quality;
- initiative/innovation;
- confidence;
- learning.

Such behaviours will lead to greater connectivity, better communication, improved systems and more empowerment. These types of behaviours already exist within most healthcare organisations but have often been stifled over the years by a controlling management style. An organisation must revitalise its staff by transforming the context in which they work. What are the foundations of a healthy culture?

- Stretch: clarity and consensus around why the organisation exists and what its aims are.
- Trust: the extent to which the actions of leaders are perceived to be fair, consistent and capable.

- Discipline: getting things done.
- Support: enabling things to happen.
  The characteristics that contribute towards a
  sense of stretch, trust, discipline and support are
  listed in the box above. . .

I shall spare you the 'box above' – the human mind can stand only so much. The upshot of it seems to be that Dr Bevington thinks people will do a better job if they are trusted, motivated and pushed a bit. Well, yes. The only thing I've ever run is a bath, but I rather think I'd worked that out for myself.

The point is not so much what he says but the way that he says it. I try to imagine my grotesquely overworked GP coming across that little gem in her *Health Service Journal* and wondering what the hell is going on in the NHS. As for the young hospital doctors trying to get on with their jobs, they must have felt like some of my BBC colleagues at the height of the Birt Terrors.

John Birt (Lord Birt now) is a clever man who did some good things for the BBC when he was the director general. But he drove many of my colleagues to distraction with his management style. We had a hint of it when he was interviewed by Brian Walden just after joining the BBC. His answer to Walden's first question was something like: 'Ah, Brian, the answer to that question comes under three headings.' We should have known there and then that it was time to head for the hills. When Greg Dyke took over, the first thing he did was announce that it was time to 'cut the crap'. And then he went on to set up his own process called 'Making It Happen', which was, in its own matey way, just as full of meaningless management jargon, and produced glossy little brochures to tell everyone what had been decided. Peter Donaldson, who reads the news on Radio Four with such authority, promptly dumped his in the bin. Then – a brave man, Peter – he wrote to Dyke to tell him he'd done so. 'I was following your advice,' he said, 'and cutting the crap.' He did not, to the best of my knowledge, receive a reply from Dyke.

I have never understood why you need to keep telling an organisation that lives or dies by its creativity that it needs to be creative. Or innovative. Or have values. Or 'commit to, and engage with, quality'. Try applying the 'opposite' test again. 'We must *not* commit to quality'? I don't think so.

Aren't I Clever!

It makes you long for Clement Attlee, the prime minister who gave us the NHS. It was said of him that he would never use one word when none would do. I try to imagine him reading Dr Bevington's golden prose. What would he have made of a word such as 'connectivity'? It is just about acceptable for technical types to use when they are describing what a computer can do, but that's it.

There are worse, though. How about 'connexity'? No, I had no idea what it meant either but it's the title of a book by a very smart man called Geoff Mulgan. He founded the Demos think tank and once ran the policy unit at No. 10, which told Tony Blair what to think. The word does exist. The *Oxford English Dictionary* confirms that it was first used in 1603 – and not, I suspect, since. Why would anyone want to resurrect it?

The answer can only be because it invites us to think that there is a meaning in all this, something erudite and really, really important that we haven't yet managed to catch up with for ourselves. It puts the author on a pedestal and the rest of us in our place. I would love to know how many doctors and nurses are intimately familiar with the work of Mannion and Ghoshal and Bartlett, referred to so comically by Dr Bevington. Sadly, a few will feel bullied into thinking they should be.

Jonathon Fielden is the deputy chairman of the BMA's consultants committee. I heard him being interviewed on the *World at One*. He used the phrase 'delivering care to the patients' (or a variant of it) no fewer than six times. The interview lasted two and a half minutes. I don't know about you, but I'm not sure I needed to be told that doctors existed to 'deliver' care, any more than you'd need to be told that bus drivers are required to propel the vehicle forward. Forget I just wrote that. Someone might start using it.

It's funny on one level but serious on another. I don't want doctors to be a 'delivery' mechanism. Language of that sort puts a barrier between doctor and patient. What is wrong with simply 'caring'?

The language of education is, if anything, worse.

Mumbo Jumbo

It starts at the top, with the stuff bureaucrats write to explain government policy. These sentences come from the government's white paper on the future of higher education:

> We see a higher education sector which meets the needs of the economy in terms of trained people, research and technology transfer. At the same time it needs to enable all suitably qualified individuals to develop their potential both intellectually and personally, and to provide the necessary storehouse of expertise in science and technology, and the arts and humanities which defines our civilisation and culture.

Note the identifying marks of bureaucracy-speak: the all-purpose 'in terms of', which keeps vague the nature of the relationship. There is a budding cliché: 'storehouse of expertise'. And watch out for this one: 'We see X . . . at the same time as Y . . .' This all-embracing construction is clever: it means that no one has any real idea where priorities may lie.

The Cambridge academic Stephan Collini did a marvellous job in the *London Review of Books* satirising how such prose could come about. He imagined a room in Whitehall 'where these collages are assembled':

> As the findings from the latest survey of focus groups come in, an official cuts out all those things which earned a positive rating and glues them together in a straight line. When a respectable number of terms have been accumulated in this way, s/he puts a dot at the end and calls it a sentence.

This mumbo-jumbo, combined with all the jargon and acronyms of Sats, Ofsted, Key Stages and so on, contaminates our schools as superbugs contaminate our hospitals. Hence the stuff I quoted in the first chapter about 'skills triplets', candidates being 'hot-seated', 'Individual Extended Contributions' and the like, sent by examining bodies to teachers and which cause my teacher friend to feel that her soul is being destroyed.

All this has not gone unchallenged. The writers Simon Gray, Selina Hastings and Anthony Thwaite kicked up early in 2004, accusing civil servants at the Department of Education of 'crimes against the English language'. Their evidence was the prose of a departmental skills guide sent to schools to help in the teaching of English to teenagers. It contained this sort of thing:

> Support is focused in the core subjects of English, mathematics and science together with other language-rich subjects as humanities and RE. Departments have to bid in for support, making clear their commitment to the work and nature of development required.

Inevitably the bug of mangled English and business jargon is caught by teachers themselves. A friend of mine wrote an email to her ten-year-old daughter's drama school, complaining that things had not been quite as they should. This was the reply she got:

> Dear Helen,
> Thankyou [sic] for your email. I have always welcomed, and encouraged, parental 'feedback' as

it's an essential quality assurance mechanism. I'm genuinely sorry that Sarah hasn't enjoyed the high quality drama experience which is my intention.

We all know that we should never go near a hospital if we want to stay well. It's beginning to seem that we should never go near a school (or at least an 'educationist') if we want to use English properly. The flat, stale language that derives from business is even being *taught* to the children. A man who marks English tests that are part of the national curriculum wrote to me:

> Two years ago, in black and white, in all seriousness it seems, in the Key Stage 3 national test for English there was a question about 'positive and negative' ways with pets. I was marking the work the children did. So I had to be tolerant with stuff like: 'I am positive when I feed my dog.' 'I am a bit negative about taking him for walks.' What was this question setter thinking?

What indeed.

All bureaucracy falls prey to language that is 'implemented' rather than spoken or written. It is inevitable because that's what bureaucrats do: they implement processes rather than engage in original thought. That is their job – and an important job it is too. The scary thing is that so much of our world is now in the grip of bureaucracy that their impenetrable, cliché-ridden language is spreading – even to those areas you might have thought would be immune.

Let's Innovate

Jeremy and Anne are champions of the delivery of innovative arts practices. I know that because I read it in a glossy programme for arto4, a conference organised by the Arts Council of the North West of England. A speaker at the conference was my colleague Alan Yentob who, I learned, is 'the focal point for talent management across the BBC'. The programme was littered with words that could have come straight from a company's annual report: 'commitment'; 'challenge'; 'significant'; 'showcase' (as a verb, naturally); 'excellence'. On and, tediously, on. And they have a set of buzz words of their own. Any modern work of art worth its salt has to be 'radical' and most of all 'risky'. There may be a perfectly simple explanation for this. The arts rely on subsidy and most of that subsidy comes from businesses. So they speak in a language of which business people will approve – even if it means nothing.

How can you be a 'champion of the delivery of

innovative arts practice'? What exactly do Jeremy
and Anne do to qualify? Perhaps they wander from
garret to garret shouting in that inane way American television audiences do when they are encouraging the participants of particularly silly game shows
on to acts of even greater stupidity. 'Yeah, Tracey!'
Or 'Woo . . . wooo . . . Love those dirty bed sheets!'
Or perhaps 'Way to go, Damien!' I doubt it. They'd
probably get Damien's pickled sharks thrust down
their throats if they tried.

No, they probably offer perfectly sensible encour-
agement to young artists who need a bit of help. So
why not say so? For the same reason, I suppose,
that those who write this sort of stuff use absurdly
inflated language to describe everything else they
and their artists do. Nick, for instance, 'works with
a diverse range of media from glass engravings to
new media art and continually asks questions about
the role of the artist . . .' Continually, eh? You
wonder he finds the time to produce any art. Then
there's Gavin, who goes one better. He 'managed
throughout his career to make artworks that critique the art world'. 'Critique' is so much classier
than 'question', don't you find? Speaking for myself
I'd like to whack the writer with that dead shark
for turning another perfectly good noun into a verb.
Then there is this:

In *Inside the White Cube*, Gormley has placed three body forms built up from individual cubes of steel. These crouching, lying and standing sculptures are placed in an orthogonal configuration within the white room. Once again, the viewer is invited to negotiate a space, but this time activated not through an implied movement but through the still presence of three works that act as a kind of residue, the indexical memory of a human space in space.

Antony Gormley has done some great things. It is hard to think of the north-east now without the image of his *Angel of the North* coming to mind. But the marketing types do him no favours by writing that sort of rubbish about his work. That piece – a press release for an exhibition – included such phrases as 'disrupting the Cartesian authority of a single-point perspective' and 'the starting point for a phenomenological or "psycho-spatial" experience'. Can it mean anything to anyone except the tiny minority who routinely use such language? Maybe that's the point. Maybe they are so pleased with themselves that there is no room in their world for sadly ignorant souls like you (perhaps) and me (certainly). Or maybe it needs a little boy to point out that the king is wearing no clothes. Or maybe I'm just missing the irony.

My Bed

Try this for a theory. Conceptual art – the sort of dreary, 'meaning-lite' rubbish that delights the headline writers every time the shortlist for the Turner Prize is published – could not exist without the pretentious language that accompanies it. Or, rather, it might still exist but nobody would pay any attention to it because they wouldn't have the first idea what to make of it. The art is validated by its description.

Watch the visitors to a modern art gallery. They will spend at least as much time reading the explanatory texts printed in little frames alongside the works as they do looking at the works themselves – sometimes more. Then they will nod wisely, glance again at the work, and move on. Or they will shake their heads and wonder if they are being had. They probably are and they probably know it, but they will look wise just in case. You never know, perhaps that unmade bed really is a work of genius.

I know Tracey Emin is an easy target for those of us who can't make head or tail of her work and I promise I'm not being unkind to her just because she described me on television as the rudest man in Britain. As it happens, I rather like her. It's just her work that baffles me. But, like it or not, *My Bed* became one of the most famous pieces of conceptual art of the past decade and the question is why. Read this though and you start to see that the work is less pretentious than what is written about it. It's by Deborah Cherry of Sussex University:

> The linen is both rumpled and smoothed, bright white and stained; beside the soiled items are pristine objects such as the glistening clear glass of the vodka bottles. If encountered in daily life, all these items would exude distinctive and powerful smells: sweaty feet, stinky ashtrays, stale body fluids of semen, blood or urine. But *My Bed* emits no strong odour. Nevertheless a stink metaphor, already in circulation for Emin's art, drifted around *My Bed*. Neal Brown's earlier celebration of her art as an 'undeodorised song of poetic extremity' (1998, 4) returned in the *Guardian*'s headline, its comparisons to Mary Kelly (the nappy liners of *Post-Partum Document*) and to Mike Kelley (besmirched toy animals and stained blankets), and its declaration (Burn, 1999, 2–3) that *My Bed* 'taps into a tradition of filth and got it dead right'. Such statements place *My Bed* in a supplementary economy of excess, that of dirt which, adding to and abutting discourses on femininity, heightened sensations of transgression swirling around Emin and her art.

As I say, it's easy to poke fun at this sort of

tosh. But why not? If someone tries to con you into thinking that there is more to something than meets the eye, why should they not be taken to task for it? And if they really believe some of this guff – a 'supplementary economy of excess'? – well, then, we have a duty to save them from themselves.

My own justification for being so snooty is that they are making a monkey of the English language. Tracey Emin once got very cross with me for failing to appreciate that art is what she says it is, so I reckon I am entitled to tell the poseurs who write about her work that English is what I say it is. And they should leave it alone.

A final word on art and language. Keith Water-house, one of our truly great columnists, is also a talented screenwriter. He once worked on a Hitch-cock film starring Paul Newman and Julie Andrews. This was in the days when Brando had made himself a huge star and the Stanislavsky method of acting was all the rage. Hitchcock thought it was nonsense. Newman did not and one scene, says Waterhouse, was giving him trouble. Newman had to meet Andrews in East Berlin and she had to place a pack-age in his hands. He approached Hitchcock:

'Hitch, it seems to me I have a situation here with Julie, I have a situation with the package, I have a situation with being in East Berlin and I have a situation with the problem of our being observed. Now how should I be relating in this scene?'

Hitchcock listened courteously and responded thus: 'Well, Mr Newman, I'll tell you exactly what I have in mind here. Miss Andrews will come down the stairs with the package, d'you see, when you, if you'll be so good, will glance just a little to the right of camera to take in her arrival. Whereupon my audience will say: "Hullo! What's this fellow looking at?" And then I'll cut away, d'you see, and show them what you're looking at.'

I have never much enjoyed Hitchcock's films but any man who can cut through cant like that deserves a cartload of Oscars.

Academic Licence

If there is one group that should be guarding and even championing the connection between language and thought it is the academic community. We employ them to think and to express what they think in language that clearly conveys the thought. But is that what they do? A friend of mine who has to read a lot of the stuff claims to be able to pick a book almost at random from his shelves, turn to any page and come up with something ghastly. So I asked him to do it. And this is what he produced.

Thane Rosenbaum's novel *Second Hand Smoke* (like Toni Morrison's *Beloved*) may be read as suggesting to historians and other analysts the need for a closer, critical examination of the intergenerational transmission of trauma and compulsively haunting experiences, or revenants, related to forms of oppression and victimization. In its parodic and self-parodic dimensions, *Second Hand Smoke* may be read as posing the ethicopolitical question of the use of humour in coming to terms with a fraught past.

That's from a new book called *History in Transit – Experience, Identity, Critical Theory* by Professor Dominick LaCapra at Cornell University. I wonder what he makes of Dostoevsky. In *The Brothers Karamazov*, Mitya and Alyosha are talking about an article written by an intellectual called Rakitin:

Mitya hurriedly pulled a piece of paper from his waistcoat pocket and read: '"In order to resolve this question it is necessary, first of all, to put one's person in conflict with one's actuality." Do you understand that?'

'No, I don't,' said Alyosha.

He was watching Mitya and listened to him with curiosity.

'I don't understand it either. Obscure and vague,

but intelligent. "Everybody writes like that now," Rakitin says, "because it's that sort of environment . . .""'

These days, much academic work seems to be written in 'that sort of environment'. It may be the pressure the academics are under. They have to churn the stuff out for the sake of their reputations – not to mention their jobs. The government has created something called the Research Assessment Exercise, which measures the amount of research published – so much easier than measuring its quality. One casualty may be the language.

Bewitching Gobbledegook

Some academics are aware of the problem and some suspect that bewitching us is exactly what their more unscrupulous colleagues are up to. Here is Gary Day, principal lecturer in English at De Montfort University, writing in the *Times Higher Educational Supplement*:

> You don't just acquire a reputation by snuffling out a topic that no one has ever heard of, you must also make it hard for your reader to know what you are talking about. There's no greater way to win the respect of your peers than to write in gobbledegook.

The less they understand the more clever they think you are.

A wise man. They do it for much the same reason that priests enjoyed speaking Latin to congregations who could not understand a word of it. If people do not understand what you are saying they cannot prove it to be nonsense. It is all of a piece with those cartels that are said to exist in academia. The 'members' agree to quote each other's work so that they can all gain Brownie points – whether anyone understands them or not.

Every so often academics with a sense of humour decide to see how far they can push the system. An American physicist, Alan Sokal, is not kind about the stuff passed off as serious academic work in less rigorous disciplines such as the humanities. He believes it is often drivel. He was particularly incensed by some of the work being done in the field of critical theory, so he submitted an article for an academic journal, *Social Text*, published by Duke University. It was called: 'Transgressing the Boundaries: Towards a Transformative Hermeneutics of Quantum Gravity'. An impressive title, you will agree. It was meaningless too. The article was gobbledegook from beginning to end – but the editors published every word of it. Game, set and match to Dr Sokal, then? Don't you believe it.

When he revealed his jolly jape, the editors were not in the least abashed. On the contrary, they said, they had known exactly what they were doing and were right to do it. As one of their defenders put it, their purpose was 'to encourage adventurism in ideas as the way to keep the intellectual pot boiling'. I leave you to ponder on how demonstrable nonsense can do that.

Lewis Carroll would approve of all this. The characters who inhabited the world that Alice discovered on the other side of the looking-glass were sane and rational compared with some of the academics who occupy the world of post-modernism. When the Red Queen said it 'takes all the running you can do to stay in the same place', Carroll thought he was getting her to talk nonsense, but you'd be surprised at how many respectable academics use it as the basis for fancy theories.

Compare Her Red Majesty with, for instance, the radical feminist academic Sandra Harding of the University of Delaware, who has written that Isaac Newton's *Principia Mathematica* is a 'rape manual'. And here's another, Luce Irigaray:

Is $E=mc^2$ a sexed equation? Perhaps it is. Let us make the hypothesis that it is insofar as it privileges the speed of light over other speeds that are vitally necessary to us. What seems to us the possibly sexed nature of this equation is not directly its uses by nuclear weapons, rather it is having privileged what goes fastest.

Not even Lewis Carroll would have tried to get away with that. But it has its defenders in this strange world. Here is what John Sturrock wrote about Irigaray in the *London Review of Books*:

> ... in that libertarian province of the intellectual world in which she functions, far better wild and contentious theses of this sort than the stultifying rigour so inappropriately demanded by Sokal.

No doubt you need a strong sense of irony to appreciate the pleasures of the language of postmodernism.

If it is amusement rather than enlightenment you are after, I recommend you type the words 'The Post-modernism Generator' into a search engine next time you are on the world-wide web. There you will find hundreds of totally bogus academic articles generated by a computer program, complete with footnotes and academic references to make them all seem authentic. They have wonderful titles such as:

'Cultural presemanticist theory in the works of Fellini'

'Reading Debord: Objectivism, neodialectic discourse and Derridaist reading'

'The Defining Characteristic of Narrative: Neoconstructive narrative in the works of Smith'

And they are all total gobbledegook. It's wonderful fun. At least it is until you realise these spoof essays are indistinguishable from what often passes for the real thing.

Remember Samantha from that saucy television programme *Sex and the City*? She makes an appearance in a scholarly work by Kim Akass and Janet McCabe called *Reading Sex and the City*. It contains some profound thoughts on the 'vulval symbolism' (yes, really) of Samantha's clothes. Each of her shoes 'enables the wearer to access, in a Lacanian sense, a more ideal and complete version of herself'. Stop giggling! This sort of stuff is being studied by students in a university somewhere near you.

But the real exploiters of gobbledegook are the personal gurus – the people who presume to tell us how to live our lives. You might think that any sensible person would run a mile from the very idea, but no. Bill Clinton was said to swear by the guidance of a 'personal development guru' called Stephen Covey.

Covey is, apparently, a leading authority on

empowerment. Among much else, he wrote an 'inspirational guide' called *The Seven Habits of Highly Effective People*. He offers 'holistic, integrated, principle-centred' solutions. Not everyone qualifies to take advantage of his advice. Don't even think of seeking it unless you are a high achiever with a 'deep need for personal congruency'.

I'd hate to give the end away, but you might like to know that 'the main thing is to keep the main thing the main thing'. Oh . . . and on the Maturity Continuum the current social paradigm enthrones independence. So that explains Bill Clinton, then. I think.

CHAPTER TEN

Danger! Politicians Speaking!

The first question *Today* presenters are asked is what time they get up in the morning. The second question is why. Why would anyone get up in the middle of the night (it's not morning: the sun hasn't even begun to rise) to go and argue with politicians? The answer, in my case, is that I love arguing. I will argue about the causes of war or the shape of the economy or how many beans make five. Arguing is fun. It is also important. At the core of democracy must be the idea that political leaders argue things out in front of the rest of us. Then we decide who has the better case and deserves our vote. Interviewing is a part of that process.

Contrary to popular belief, not all political interviews on *Today* are aggressive or even, to use that more limp-wristed word, robust. But some are — and so they should be. Political interviewing is mostly about challenging claims and testing arguments. Left to their own devices, politicians will repeat the same point to distraction and use the interview as a party political broadcast. This might even mean – heaven forfend – having to interrupt occasionally.

I like politicians and I sometimes feel sorry for them. Theirs is a hellish job. There is no consolation prize for the good loser: you either succeed or you fail and, sooner or later, all politicians fail. The prize for coming first is the end of any hope of a normal life. The pressures on a party leader or cabinet minister are quite extraordinary and you wonder why any rational human being could possibly want to do it.

Ordinary people live in a world of worries about real things: mortgages, hospital waiting lists and trying to get the kids into a decent school. Politicians in power live in a world of meetings where initiatives and action plans are discussed and promises considered. They use a different language from the rest of us. It is a world where all the talk is of concrete steps or, these days, step changes; levelling playing-fields (if they haven't all been sold to supermarkets); windows of opportunity waiting to be looked through; track records to establish; hymn sheets to be sung from; learning curves to be mastered; long grass for balls to be kept out of; steep hills to climb (never gradual inclines); clear blue water to be maintained; green lights to be given and so on.

The first few times these metaphors are used they may have real force. David Mellor, the culture secretary under John Major, warned the press they were 'drinking in the last-chance saloon' after some infringement of privacy. It was clear what he meant: if they didn't stop it, there would be laws to make them. Over the years the phrase entered the vocabulary. Like so many others, it has become tired and worn and is hauled out of the lexicon of political cliché when its users can't be bothered to find a better way of saying what needs to be said.

It would be good to draw a line under all this. But what sort of line? Should it be a thin line or a red line or maybe a thin red line or even a line in the sand? That last one has always puzzled me. Won't the tide wash the line away? Maybe that's the idea.

I'm blessed if I can tell the difference between them all – and I deal with this stuff every day. Heaven help the poor old punter who was never really interested in politics in the first place. Faced with this dead, uninspiring language it's hardly surprising that he switches off.

In the Hen House

Philip Roth says that when he hears George W. Bush speak he hears a ventriloquist. Nearly sixty years earlier George Orwell made a similar observation about political language in general. Here is what he said in his *Politics and the English Language*:

> When one watches some tired hack on the platform mechanically repeating the familiar phrases – *bestial atrocities, iron heel, blood-stained tyranny, free peoples of the world, stand shoulder to shoulder* – one often has a curious feeling that one is not watching a live human being but some kind of dummy: a feeling which suddenly becomes stronger at moments when the light catches the speaker's spectacles and turns them into blank discs which seem to have no eyes behind them.

Ah, yes, 'stand shoulder to shoulder'. There's one that has not gone away. It came to define our relationship with the United States in what we must now think of as the 'post 9/11 era'. Orwell's essay goes on:

> As soon as certain topics are raised, the concrete melts into the abstract and no one seems able to think of turns of speech that are not hackneyed:

prose consists less and less of *words* chosen for the sake of their meaning, and more of *phrases* tacked together like the sections of a prefabricated hen-house.

This notion of words being used by politicians independently of any connection with meaning or thought was described even more caustically by Senator William McAdoo in an attack on President Warren Harding:

His speeches leave the impression of an army of pompous phrases moving over the landscape in search of an idea. Sometimes these meandering words would actually capture a straggling thought and bear it triumphantly, a prisoner in their midst, until it died of servitude and overwork.

Matthew Parris, a Tory MP who left politics for journalism, quotes that with obvious relish in his anthology of insults, *Scorn*. He has met one or two Hardings in his time. It is an arresting thought: words in search of a meaning instead of the other way about. Sometimes we don't notice it is happening: we are too worn down to make the effort. This comes from the preface to *The Blair Revolution*, the book Peter Mandelson and Roger Liddle published the year before New Labour came to power.

The principal challenges are to overcome Britain's continued slide in international competitiveness so as to create a successful economy based on partnership between the private and public sectors, and to create a more equal and cohesive society, less scarred by division and want, and capable of providing the opportunities every family rightly aspires to.

You can smell the straw (or something more pungent) of Orwell's hen house in this. At first glance there is nothing obviously wrong with the sentence – give or take a few commas in the wrong place. All the buzz words are there: 'partnership . . . equal . . . cohesive society . . . opportunities'. But then you realise what Orwell meant when he wrote about tacking phrases together rather than choosing them carefully according to their meaning. That's what Mandelson and Liddle have done, and the result is like one of those Ikea self-assembly packs when you can't follow the instructions: they've put the roof where the floor should be. We don't need to become more competitive to create a successful economy. The reverse is true. The sentence makes sense only if you turn it upside down. Here's how it should have read to make any sense at all:

The principal challenges are to create a successful economy based on partnership between the public and private sectors so as to overcome Britain's slide in international competitiveness, and . . .

Then there's the business of separating words from their meaning altogether. Here's an example from the same book:

New Labour's distinctive emphasis is on its concept of community. This is not a soft, romantic concept . . . Community is a robust and powerful idea . . . It means teamwork . . . It means mutuality . . . It means justice . . .

Few people would argue with the broad sentiment that community is a good thing. But it does not 'mean justice'. When villagers in the Middle Ages got together and decided someone was a witch they were certainly acting as a community. But I doubt that as old Rebecca drowned on the ducking stool she felt she had been dealt with justly.

To Verb or Not to . . .

Verbs cement sentences to their meaning so it's not too surprising that politicians tend to mistrust them. Tony Blair is one of the many who seem wary of verbs. His early speeches were famous for the number of sentences without them. Simon Hoggart of the *Guardian*, who identified the phenomenon and has become the world's leading expert in the field, counted 163 verbless sentences in Blair's 2000 conference speech – an Olympic record, he claimed. You know the sort of thing: 'New challenges, new ideas.' 'The future, not the past.' 'New Labour, new ideas.' 'The age of achievement, at home and abroad.' 'Hope.' 'Opportunity.' 'For our young people, a brighter future.' It makes for good rhetoric. I have watched the delegates in the conference hall responding to it and applauding wildly. Then I have spoken to them afterwards and many seemed a little uncertain as to what it all meant. That's the way it is with conference speeches. You get carried away with the rhetoric and atmosphere and try to make sense of it later.

Hoggart had great fun with one of Blair's metaphors: 'This is a journey worth making and a fight worth fighting.' He thought it could as easily apply to football hooligans, who believe no journey is worthwhile without a fight: 'We shall hurl the bar stool of opportunity through the plate-glass window of privilege.'

The point about verbs is that they commit the speaker. To declaim 'New Labour, new members!' is not the same as saying, 'We have new members,' or 'We are committed to signing up new members.' It could mean either or both or neither. It could be just a vague aspiration. When Tory leaders use 'Lower taxes' as a sentence it means nothing. If they include a verb, such as 'promise', they are committed to a course of action. Without the verb there is no commitment, but the phrase must be used because that is what Tory leaders are expected to say. When politicians do use verbs the choice can be revealing. Policies are generally 'put in place'. It is a strangely static notion. You put exhibits in place in an exhibition and there they stay – to be admired but not touched. Perhaps at some level that is how politicians see their policies: they are there to be unveiled and admired. Just don't expect anything to happen.

'Agenda' is another favourite word in ministers' offices and there's nothing wrong with it – except when they try to find verbs to keep it company. You cannot 'move forward' an agenda, which is what one minister said needed to be done, any more than you can 'drive' one. That's what Messrs Chirac, Schroeder and Blair told us they were doing when they ended a summit in Berlin. But Keith Vaz, the former Europe minister, clearly gets much more excited by agendas. He complained to *Newsnight*, 'We are dancing to the wrong agenda.'

Europe ministers must spend most of their lives locked in endless meetings in Brussels committee rooms discussing vital issues such as sub-section

13a of clause two of the annexe to the Paperclips Protection Directive (2003). So it's not surprising that Mr Vaz occasionally fantasised about dancing around the room to a rousing Viennese Agenda Waltz. Which might also help explain how one of his colleagues came up with this:

> We should take up the gauntlet and run with it.

Better, I suppose, than slapping his secretary of state smartly on the cheek with it before challenging him to a waltz.

Come Drive with Me ...

By and large, politicians should avoid motoring metaphors because they end up crashing the verbs. Tony Blair once boasted that he did not have a reverse gear. A few months later he did a complete reversal on holding a referendum on the European constitution. But, then, maybe a U-turn needs no reverse gear. Shortly after that he was at it again: 'Now is not the time for a change of direction,' he said, 'but it is the time for a change of gear.' You just knew he would regret that one too. But dutiful junior ministers had already picked up that this was the current metaphor of choice, so we had this from one of them in the Department for Work and Pensions:

> We do now need perhaps to kick in a new gear change. Let's raise our game a gear. Let's really now focus upon those people who face the hardest barriers preventing them from finding work . . . I'm all in favour of us putting all our shoulders to the wheel.

It's a pity, really, that there is no prize for the greatest number of clichés in one short answer. The loser is the poor old listener who has to try to stay awake.

George Bush has done his bit for steering his motoring metaphors into a pile-up of verbs. It was he who decided that what the Middle East needed was a new peace plan. Except he didn't call it that. He called it a road map. The problem with the metaphor is that maps are for looking at but peace plans are for putting into effect. How can you put a map into effect? How can you 'implement' it, as the verb that came to be most commonly attached to the road map suggested? Once it became clear that nothing was being implemented anyway, it became necessary to find other verbs. One politician talked about 'jettisoning' bits of the road map – a rum notion if ever there was one. 'Oh dear, Doris,

I hate that stretch of the M6 when we drive up to your mother's. Shall we jettison it?' Another said, 'The broad outlines of the road map have been kicked into touch.' It could have been worse, I suppose. It could have been kicked into the long grass.

Someone on the radio (it might even have been me) said, 'The road map isn't going anywhere.' That is profoundly silly. Maps never go anywhere: they merely indicate the way. And if the map is a cock-up from the start, there is only one thing to do with it:

Bush Rips Up the Road Map.

That was the headline in the *Guardian*. Now this is something you *can* do with a map: rip it up. So the metaphor came into its own only at the point when it was clear it had to be dumped.

Like the sad story of the Middle East, it was a disaster from the start.

. . . But at Your Expense

Oddly enough, politicians don't much like the word 'money'. If, say, the libraries are so hard up they are forced to hire lap-dancers to bring in a bit of extra revenue you will never hear anyone say they are short of cash. They will say they are starved of 'resources'.

Nor do politicians spend money: they invest it. And it's always 'government' money, which, of course, does not exist. The government does not own or earn a penny. It is our money – all of it. Yet we are told (and we journalists faithfully report) that 'The government has invested an extra £5bn in something or other.' No, it hasn't. We have – whether we chose to or not. When did you last hear a Chancellor of the Exchequer say that he is 'spending another £5bn of taxpayers' money'?

I did a Hoggart-style count on Gordon Brown's 2004 Budget statement. He used the word 'investment' forty times – more often than any of his other favourite words. He used 'spending' only a few times – and then only when it referred to what we, the 'consumers', do with our money. The equation is simple: we spend; they invest.

So Gordon hasn't 'spent' any of our money for years. He has invested it. The word that usually goes with 'invest' is 'wise'. The word that usually goes with 'spend' is 'tax'. Thus the most dreaded of all political compound verbs: 'tax-and-spend'. We all know that is what governments do. Some argue that that is what they are for. But they no longer dare put it like that. The Tories accused Mr Brown of sleight-of-hand and then they joined in. Michael Howard proudly announced that a Conservative government would (you've guessed it) 'invest more to achieve reform'. I think I'll pop down the pub now and invest in a couple of pints and a bag of crisps.

But let's have another Brownism first. Mr Brown has often told us that his policies 'lock in' stability. What a curious way of putting it. Stability, at the risk of coming over all technical, is something that is created when the forces acting on a free-standing body are kept carefully in balance. Maintaining stability is about nudging those forces gently every so often to keep the balance. You wouldn't need stabilisers on a child's bicycle if it never moved. 'Locking in' suggests an inflexibility that could be economically disastrous.

In reality, the Chancellor is trying to convey something else. With him, reponsibility is sacrosanct, untouchable, locked away in a vault somewhere. His mixed metaphor tries to put two separate notions in our head – or should I say put them 'in place'?

With few exceptions, leading politicians around the world believe in capitalism. Gordon Brown is, of course, one of them. But when did you last hear them use the word in an approving sense? They don't do it. As the great economist J. K. Galbraith notes, it has been replaced everywhere by the phrase 'the market system'. Capitalism, it seems, is seen as a 'weak brand'. Galbraith regards this sort of thing as an 'innocent fraud'.

Whose Line Is It Anyway?

The first half of 2004 was a golden age for red-line enthusiasts. The lines were defended, abandoned, softened, reconsidered, renegotiated. Ministers did just about everything with them as they tried to reach agreement on the European constitution except paint them yellow and park on them. I wonder how many people beyond the corridors of Whitehall had a clue what it was all about.

Inevitably, 'red line' became a verb. Various issues affecting national sovereignty were 'red-lined'. Whatever happened to 'ring-fenced'? Just fell out of fashion, I suppose. A visitor from Mars might wonder whether political and parliamentary language is designed deliberately to keep the public in the dark. Peter Hain, the leader of the House of Commons, went public with his worries about an attempt to wreck a bill by 'long-grassing it for ever'. Here he is talking about the same bill to *The Times:*

'If the Conservative front bench incites the Lords to defy the Commons in this way we will pull the bill out of the Lords, put it into the Commons and then we will Parliament Act it.'

Put aside the dubious notion of the Lords 'defying' the Commons. Who ever said the Lords were

required to obey the Commons? The truly impressive part of that sentence is the use of 'Parliament
Act' as a verb. You can imagine the exchange in one
of those plush committee rooms.

Peter Hain: 'Behave yourself, milord, or I'll Parliament Act you!'

His Lordship: 'Oh, no, Minister, anything but
that!'

Next thing you know, Mr Hain will be threatening to whip the wretched peer. Actually, that would
not be a threat. It is *withdrawing* the whip that's a
threat in the Palace of Westminster. Confused? You
certainly would be if you tried to follow these things
too closely. The language would get you in the end.

It got to my old friend John Simpson. We worked
together in South Africa until he left to become the
BBC's political editor in London. He hated the job
and wrote regularly to me with horror stories –
mostly about how his 'colleagues' in the political
unit spent their time resenting him for being promoted above their heads and trying to do him down.
But his big problem was getting a grip on parliamentary procedure and language. He was unsettled
most, he wrote, by the enthusiasm for 'early day
motions', which reminded him of the discipline in
his days at boarding-school. He wondered whether
Mr Speaker should be replaced by Matron.

We're the Managers Now

Politicians do have a defence of sorts for the increasingly dreary (and often incomprehensible) nature of their language. Back in the days when they wore frock coats to work they saw their job largely as inspiring us with their rhetoric and getting us to see the world as they did. They had little to do except talk. But the state has grown over the centuries and now ministers run vast departments that influence almost every aspect of our lives. Try to imagine, to take just one example, a Department for Culture, Media and Sport in the Victorian age. The effect of this is that ministers have had to become managers. And the deadly virus of management-speak has infected their language.

The role of even the most ancient offices of state has changed too. The Chancellor of the Exchequer runs the economy today in a way that would have been unthinkable until relatively recently – although that has much to do with the personality of Gordon Brown. In 2004 he became the longest serving chancellor since the nineteenth century. The previous record holder was a man Mr Brown is said to admire above all other chancellors: David Lloyd George. I wonder if he ever compares the language of his hero with that of his underlings. Here is Lloyd George introducing his 'People's Budget' in 1909:

Out of the money raised by taxing superfluities, funds will be established to secure honourable sustenance for the deserving old, and to assist our great benefit societies in making adequate provisions for sickness and infirmity, and against the poverty which comes to the widows and orphans of those who fall in the battle of industry.

And here is the financial secretary to the Treasury, Ruth Kelly, nearly a century later:

'It brings us to the forefront of best practice.'

I know that's a bit unfair. Lloyd George was announcing an historic social reform and Ms Kelly was merely commending some Treasury action or other. And, anyway, no modern politician would get away with a phrase like 'falling in the battle of industry'. The Health and Safety Executive would have their guts for garters. Who was responsible for so many people falling? Was the floor slippery? Someone must be held to account. There must be transparency.

Or imagine Lloyd George coming out with 'post-neoclassical endogenous growth theory', as Gordon Brown once did. As we all know, Mr Brown was much mocked for the high-falutin' phrase – famously by Michael Heseltine, who pointed out that it had been coined by his faithful servant Ed Balls and thus 'It wasn't Brown's: it was Balls!' Years later Mr Balls told us that all it really meant was that the government can make a difference to the economy. I prefer the original. Much classier.

Powerful rhetoric can have a lasting effect. No one who was there in 1985 will forget Neil Kinnock's scorching attack on the Militant Tendency people who had infiltrated the Labour Party in Liverpool:

> 'You start with far-fetched resolutions . . . pickled into a rigid dogma . . . and you end in the grotesque chaos of a Labour council – a Labour council – hiring taxis to scuttle round a city handing out redundancy notices to its own workers.'

On paper the repetition of 'a Labour council' looks clumsy. When he spoke the words they dripped with scorn. It was the beginning of the end for Militant. But Mr Kinnock never made it into government and it is not until politicians have to start running things that their language becomes permeated with the worst of the dreary, soulless, often meaningless rubbish that passes for communication at sales seminars and the like.

It makes you feel that you have mistakenly opened the door to a man with a shiny black briefcase who wants your house to become a showcase for the most sensational double-glazing and if you agree you will have to pay only half the real value in easy instalments. There is only one thing to do: slam the door quickly.

This Is Geometry?

'Envelope' is a favourite business word – although, obviously, it has nothing to do with what you put letters in. If you are a thrusting, go-ahead executive it is vital that you are seen to push the envelope. I believe – but don't hold me to this – that it is almost as important as thinking outside the box. Bureaucrats like envelopes too, which is why the EU Agricultural Council came up with the need for a 'restructuring envelope'. That produced this little gem, when the Institute for Fiscal Studies helpfully told us what the Tories intended doing with the 'overall envelope for public spending':

> Mr Letwin is talking about cutting the overall envelope from 42 per cent to 40 per cent . . .

What conceivable value can a metaphor like that hold? Does it make it easier for anyone – even an experienced economist – to understand what is being discussed? We put things into an envelope and cut it open to take them out. The image could scarcely be less helpful. But jargon respects no known laws of nature.

The European Union excels at this sort of thing. One former Europe minister for France described the relationship that should exist between her own country, Germany, and Britain:

> A new form of triangular *entente cordiale* with variable geometry, which could become a square or a pentagon later.

But of course, the *new* form! Why didn't we think of that earlier, instead of getting hung up on the *old* form every time we discussed triangular *entente cordiale* with variable geometry over a beer down the local? Put like that it is so obvious. But what if things go wrong? Don't panic. If a gremlin gets into the works and the whole thing starts going haywire, with klaxons and sirens warning that the pentagon is about to self-destruct or become a multi-faceted tetrahedron ... well, there's the 'emergency brake mechanism' to apply. Eurocrats love their brake so much they have now developed a 'brake augmented by enhanced cooperation'. Thank God for that. We can all sleep a little easier in our beds at night knowing it is there.

Diplomacy can be tricky. Countries guard their own interests jealously and the wording of international agreement and negotiation needs to be precise. But we might all have a better idea of what is going on if the diplomats were to use language when they talk to us mere mortals that we have a fighting chance of understanding. It might be, of course, that they would prefer we were kept in the dark.

They know that many people are suspicious of the power exercised from Brussels, so what do they do? They drop the word 'power' and substitute 'competence'. Somehow it sounds less threatening. Thus, the new constitution refers to 'shared competencies' instead of shared power.

If you are truly masochistic you might try reading the constitution and the documents surrounding it, then working out what it all means. The word 'pertannually' occurs in clause 82, paragraph 17, subsection (b) of the original treaty. Puzzled by that? Don't worry. We are advised that it has been deleted and replaced with the word 'insubdurience'. So that's all right, then.

I am afraid we are back in the world of Alice and Humpty Dumpty – only more so. If no one understands this stuff, apart from the pointy-heads who wrote it, everyone can claim it means what they want it to mean. Remember, Kenneth Clarke admitted he had not even read the Maastricht Treaty – and he was in the cabinet at the time.

Wanna be Ofsteded?

The virus of jargon-ridden managerial language is at its worst in education. It gets into politicians' linguistic bloodstream and they find themselves parroting it. In the row over university top-up fees, one MP got up in the House of Commons and shouted angrily:

'Universities don't need to be Ofsted-ed!'

In Simon Hoggart's view – and he has to spend his life listening to the stuff – 'whole areas of parliamentary life have been ethnically cleansed of the English tongue'. Here he is reporting on education questions in the House of Commons back in 1999, when David Blunkett was still education secretary.

David Blunkett, the secretary of state, told us that he hoped 'to extend the intensification of the gateway'. Something or other was 'co-terminous with the learning and skills councils'. In the world inhabited by Mr Blunkett and his junior ministers, nobody ever borrows more books. Instead there is a 'massive take-up of the library service' . . .

Mr Michael Wills, another junior minister, was asked about 'enhanced services at the gateway stage'. He replied, to everyone's apparent satisfaction, that

the government had 'established trailblazer pro-
jects'. This delighted a backbencher, Rosie Win-
terton, who said that she supported trailblazer
initiatives 'because of the help it will give in best-
practice coalition with employers'.

To them it is as straightforward as the Gettysburg
Address. Mr Wills continued, 'The point is to
promote best practice for the roll-out when they
emerge into their own gateways, promoting the soft
skills that employers want to see.' You expect someone to shout out: 'For Gawd's sake, speak English,
can't you?' But no one does.

David Miliband, said to possess one of the biggest
brains in the Labour government, was schools minister when he came up with this jaw-dropper:

> 'The time is right to embed honest, hard-edged
> self-evaluation across the system . . . which needs
> to be data-rich and workload light.'

Surely Mr Miliband knows that you don't embed
things 'across': you embed them 'in'. But that is
a minor infringement compared with the broader
indictment. The sentence is meaningless.

Incidentally 'the time is right' is a little verbal
trick much loved by politicians. It is another way of
distancing themselves from the actions. Instead of

saying, 'Look, money is a bit short and I can't think of anything else to do so I'm going to covert all our primary schools into casinos', they say, 'The time is right'. So let's blame the time. They do it in reverse too: 'This is no time for . . .' The classic usage is 'This is no time for complacency . . .' Well, maybe not, but one of these days I want to ask the minister when *is* the time for complacency. Is there a target date by which complacency must be embedded across the system?

Out of the Mouths . . .

Because they have so many things to manage, one of the things ministers cannot do is write all their own speeches. Their diaries are packed with engagements and everywhere they go they are expected to say something. It might be the big speech at the national conference of whatever trade association their department deals with, or it might be 'just a few words' at some award ceremony.

Quite why they get invited to all these events is beyond me. I can understand the appeal of the prime minister or the chancellor. Even if they don't say anything very interesting – and they usually don't – they have real power and people like to be in the presence of power. But there is no great buzz to be had from an appearance by the junior minister for the Department of Things No One Else Wants to Deal With. I suppose they hope the minister will use his massive influence to provide free condoms for five-year-olds or whatever they're after. These are the tadpoles in the political pond, praying that one day they will become powerful frogs with their own seat in the cabinet pond. They attend the events because everyone else refused and they are too junior to say no. But because they are 'The Minister' they get 'The Keynote Speech' – which is itself a terrible misnomer. I have been at conferences where every session begins with a 'keynote speech' (how can there be more than one?) and have yet to discover what it means. I think it means that it is longer than all the others.

The minister's speech is written by the civil servants. Sometimes he is so busy he scarcely gets a chance to read it beforehand. I have sat next to them in the front row while they are waiting to be introduced. They scan the words they are expected to deliver with conviction and they groan. Sometimes they will mutter, very quietly, 'This is crap!' Occasionally a brave or foolhardy minister – or someone who knows he is for the chop in the next reshuffle and has nothing to lose – will throw it away and deliver a few words of his own. Mostly they just read aloud the turgid stuff that has been prepared for them with as much enthusiasm as they can muster and hope that none of the questions that follow will expose their ignorance of the subject on which they are supposed to be expert.

It is different – but not much different – at cabinet level. Secretaries of state tend to make the more important speeches, but they suffer from the same dead hands at the computer keyboards. John Reid, the health secretary at the time of writing, learned his politics in the city where the 'Glasgow kiss' was born. He is a political bruiser – clever, quick-witted, ruthless and ambitious – and when you interview him you do your homework beforehand. But listen to him in this speech talking to nurses' leaders:

'Nurses are delivering for patients and the public and we are delivering for them.'

'Ah, 'delivering' again. That is the language of the marketing consultant – or possibly nurses who specialise in midwifery – not the politician who promised to 'set out my vision'. He goes on:

'About career pathways for nurses – the chief nursing officer is getting a grip on this in her post-registration task group.'

Whoever wrote this stuff has only a fleeting acquaintance with the English language but a great command of clichéd thinking. Getting 'a grip on career pathways in a task group' is a daunting prospect, but there is worse to come:

> 'The challenge is . . . how to liberate you from the remnants of the old ways of thinking. The answer, I think, is to encourage a new generation of entrepreneurial nurses.'

Let us allow 'challenge' to go unchallenged. I believe there is now a by-law that says the word must be included at least fourteen times in every speech that also contains the word 'vision'. 'Values' must get a dozen mentions. Naturally the use of 'problem' has been banned: uplifting language only allowed. I can offer you no help with the notion of being liberated from a remnant, but the word that demands a little attention in that passage is 'entrepreneurial'. In fairness to the speech-writer, Dr Reid does acknowledge that entrepreneurial nurses may seem an odd concept. He tries to justify it with this:

> 'Being an entrepreneur means being prepared to take some risks.'

Remember that next time you are in hospital. Nurses should take risks. And there was I assuming that good nursing was about helping to eliminate risks. But all is explained in the next sentences:

'Nurses who will on every occasion, at every time, recognise that this person is different from the last patient and needs something new, something different that will ensure better care. It is about using the opportunities of our investment in the NHS to create new ways for nursing to do what it does best – within the values of the NHS.'

This is extraordinary language. Words are being borrowed but their meanings left behind. It turns out that 'risk' in this context means treating every patient differently and taking initiatives. But isn't that what every good nurse has done with every patient since Florence Nightingale trimmed her first wick? What does it have to do with what any normal person would understand by the word 'risk'? And how does a nurse 'use the opportunities of our investment'? Search me. Anyway, at the risk of labouring the point, it's not the government's investment. It's the taxpayers'.

What this is all about is commandeering a vocabulary for effect rather than meaning. I have no idea what effect it had on Dr Reid's audience, but the nurses' leader, Beverly Malone, did say some months later that she was worried that some nurses were becoming 'too posh to wash'. Maybe that's because they see themselves as entrepreneurs. Successful entrepreneurs would get others to do the washing for them and make a profit on the deal.

It's the Thought that Counts

I feel a bit guilty picking on John Reid. Thousands of speeches are churned out by the Whitehall machine every year and almost all of them would have provided rich pickings. But Dr Reid is capable of clear, simple, direct language and it seems a pity that he has to deliver this sort of meaningless guff.

The same cannot be said of John Prescott. He does not select his words with precision and assemble them with care. He uses the equivalent of a JCB, scoops them up in a vast bucket and dumps them out in a great, jumbled heap. For years Mr Prescott has been the hero of the parliamentary sketch writers, those stars of the Westminster firmament who must produce scintillating gems day after day from the dross that often passes for debate in the chamber.

Mr Prescott has saved their bacon more often than a mountain-rescue team plucks foolhardy walkers from Ben Nevis in winter. Whenever they run short of ideas and he makes an appearance at the despatch box, they know their problems are over. He can be guaranteed to produce something along these lines:

> I think, as the Right Honourable Member made clear in the debate on Monday, the judgment about President Reagan, I must say on my part whatever was said about President Reagan, and there was, I must say that in fact whatever they said about at the beginning of his regime, he did contribute to reducing the weapons of mass destruction and I think that was a contribution to the world peace.

Pluck a few sentences like that from Mr Prescott's answers, add a sarcastic comment or two and, bingo, you have a sketch. It never fails. With such rich material you may wonder why I have left it so late in this chapter on political language to turn my attentions to him. That is because he is not one of the guilty men. I am not suggesting for a moment that he would be anyone's first choice to conduct delicate negotiations on a new treaty that required subtle, deliberately ambiguous wording. His problem – and his strength – is that you know exactly what he means. Because of his difficulties with the language, Mr Prescott has never mastered the art of concealment or, by extension, manipulation. When you hear him speak without a script, you hear him think. He can be a more powerful orator because of it.

When John Smith was leader of the Labour Party he faced a critically important vote at the party conference. If he had lost, it could have cost him the leadership. John Prescott was called in at the last minute, when support was slipping away, to rally the doubters. It was an extraordinary speech, garbled, inarticulate, a grammatical wasteland – but passionate, powerful and ultimately persuasive. He won the day.

Years later we talked about it and he admitted that he had never watched a replay of his speech on videotape. I asked him why. 'Too embarrassed,' he muttered. He had no reason to be embarrassed. He did what politicians should do: he connected with his audience. They might not have followed every sentence, but they knew exactly what he meant.

Donald Rumsfeld, the American defence secretary, has an original approach to language too. This has become recognised as a gobbledegook classic:

Reports that say something hasn't happened are always interesting to me because, as we know, there are known knowns: there are things we know we know. We also know there are known unknowns; that is to say we know there are some things we do not know. But there are also unknown unknowns – the ones we don't know we don't know.

Rumsfeld won the Plain English Campaign's Foot-in-Mouth Award for that, which seems fair enough when you read it quickly. In fact, his language is exemplary: it's the thought behind it that is complicated. You just need a bit of patience to work out what he is saying. There may be many reasons to put Mr Rumsfeld in the stocks, but this is not one of them – unless it is an offence for a politician to rise above the banal. On the contrary, he should be congratulated for daring to express a complicated thought. Is the Plain English Campaign interested only in plain thought?

CHAPTER ELEVEN

Who Guards the Guardians?

There is something presumptuous – to put it charitably – about a journalist sounding off about the use of language. Whose fault is it that the language is so often mangled and manipulated? Everyone does it – politicians and business leaders, marketing people and bureaucrats – but journalists are the people who are meant to spot it and warn about it. And half the time we are just as bad.

We are meant to be the guardians, using clear, precise and simple language, cutting through the jargon and the cant, exposing duplicity and manipulation. And what do we do? Read any newspaper, listen to any news report, and you will spot the clichés, the solecisms and the clumsy language. It is like a referee in a football match ignoring blatant fouls, changing the rules throughout the game, then penalising the players because they keep breaking them. Oh . . . and then complaining because being a referee is such a tough job. Journalists do a lot of complaining.

So let's apportion the blame.

The obvious culprits are the tabloid newspapers – especially the so-called 'red-tops'. Yes, they love clichéd language. They almost invented it. Some tabloid creations have become so venerable that not even the most shameless hack will use them any longer – except in parody. The days of Ron Knee, the football manager who managed to be simultaneously ashen-faced and tight-lipped, are gone. He is, sadly, extinct – although some would argue he never existed beyond the pages of *Private Eye*. Neither are managers over the moon any longer or as sick as a parrot after a game of two halves. They have gone . . . all gone. The gorgeous pouting blonde is on the verge of extinction, although she manages to survive in spirit. Battling grannies are holding their own – but only just. So, yes, there have been casualties along the way but, no matter, there are plenty more where they came from:

- Feelings always run high.
- Doubts are always nagging.
- Warnings (and reminders) are always stark.
- Reality is always grim.
- I have yet to read of a murder that is not brutal (can a murder be gentle?) or a quarrel that is not bitter.
- Outrage is invariably strong (as against mild outrage perhaps?).

- Police with tracker dogs still comb the area.
- Daylight still reveals the charred remains.
- Wreckage is always scattered over a wide area.
- Reporters have sneak previews, even when five hundred journalists have been invited to a formal press event.
- Any house that is marginally more comfortable than a Calcutta slum is a luxury home – especially if it is owned by someone of whom the newspaper disapproves.
- Every parliamentary committee is powerful – assuming it is saying something of which the newspaper approves.
- Organisations are no longer criticised; they are named and shamed.
- Inanimate objects, such as ships or planes, suffer damage. Quite how they communicate their suffering is never explained.
- People die tragically (as opposed to joyfully).

Spotting clichés in the red-tops is great fun and also a pointless exercise. Tabloids without clichés would be like rice pudding without the skin or roast pork without crackling: they would somehow lose their character. You know where you are with an old, familiar tabloid cliché.

So where is the good English in journalism? It is in those same newspapers. The tabloids contain the best and the worst. A good leading article in a tabloid newspaper can say as much in a hundred words as a posh leader writer might say in five hundred. It was no less an authority than Hilaire Belloc who said lucidity is the 'soul of style'. The red-top leader will not be balanced and nuanced, but it's not meant to be. It will be sharp, often funny, and crystal clear. It will leave you in not the slightest doubt about what the newspaper thinks. It will never use two words where one will do and it will distil a complex argument into something straightforward and simple or, frequently, simplistic.

If you want reasoned argument you do not read the tabloids. Tabloid English is not for thinking clever thoughts: it is for cheering and booing. The tabloids, by and large, do not challenge our individual prejudices: they confirm them. If you want a judicious discussion about the problems of, say, asylum and immigration, you do not turn to the *Sun* or the *Daily Mirror*, let alone the *Daily Mail*. A good tabloid editor knows what the readers want and gives it to them. If that sounds patronising or snooty, it is not meant to be. Tabloid readers know what they are getting and they can – and do – dump the paper if it does something of which they disapprove. The *Sun* is still trying to recapture the readers it lost on Merseyside after the Hillsborough disaster when it accused Liverpool supporters (wrongly) of behaving shamefully. That was more than fifteen years ago. Readers cannot be taken for granted.

Americans who come to live in this country often tell me they are shocked by the quality of our tabloid press. It doesn't surprise me. They have been bored into submission, weaned on papers like the *New York Times*, which would not survive five minutes against the competition of even our dullest broadsheets. The *NYT* has some brilliant writing and clever contributors, but it is deeply, deeply dull. Its layout is atrocious, its headlines ponderous and its general reporting both clichéd and wordy. As for American tabloids, they have the weaknesses of British tabloids with none of their strengths.

So if we cannot blame the tabloids, what about the broadsheets? Well, they're not much better when it comes to clichés. Here is a modest sample taken over a couple of days:

- Someone or other is set on a collision course with someone else.
- Developments get the green light . . . except when they are given the go-ahead.
- Politicians seek to put clear water between their party and the other lot.
- Every report is long-awaited and almost always wide-ranging.

- Refugee camps are always makeshift.
- Famines are always Biblical.
- Warnings are always wake-up calls and the consequences of ignoring them are dire.
- Reminders are timely and doubts are always lingering.

In other words, they are just as predictable as tabloid clichés, only duller. Sometimes they will string clichés together – to bizarre effect:

- Mr Blair has reached a crossroads. Downing Street acknowledges that Iraq is the 'elephant in the bed' and will not disappear as a 'significant negative'.
- Gay couples finally got a £100m green light yesterday to start preparing for all the joys of near-marriage

The broadsheets' responsibilities are greater than the tabloids' because, unlike the red-tops, they do claim to challenge prejudice and to engage in serious argument. But the language they use can often mislead. Scientific research is a good example. It is rarely reported as 'suggesting' some truth – although that is almost always the extent of the claim being made. Instead scientists 'have discovered' or the 'research shows'. It is almost always a 'breakthrough' even when the researchers have taken pains to present their findings in a more modest light by emphasising the uncertainties and the tentative nature of any conclusions. When my colleagues on *Today* follow up the story for the (almost) obligatory 'scientific breakthrough' slot at 6.50-ish it tends to be told differently. The scientist almost always uses language that is far more restrained than the words in the newspaper version. The temptation to hype language is not restricted to the tabloids.

Alan Bennett satirised the way newspaper headlines make things sound more dramatic: 'Pope braves drizzle.'

Well, then, perhaps we should blame the broadsheet newspapers for the standard of English today. But that won't do either – any more than we should blame those novelists or playwrights or Hollywood script-writers who take appalling liberties with the language to create a particular effect. We can choose what papers we buy, what books we read, what films we see. But there is one institution that is all pervasive, whose influence cannot be ignored. It is, of course, the BBC.

The French have their Académie Française and the British have the BBC. The Académie exists to police the French language and the BBC exists to make programmes. But it probably has a far greater influence over the way we use the English language than the Académie has over the way the French use theirs.

Observe or Police?

The BBC's role in defining and determining our common language is pivotal. It delivers more words every hour of the day and night than any other organisation in the land – with the possible exception of the Civil Service. You cannot escape the BBC, no matter how hard you try. One way or another we will get you. Here is how the *Guardian* puts it:

> BBC English is often spoken of in jest, as if it were some figment of the 50s. But the official parlance of the Corporation still does have its influence. The use of a word or phrase in, say, a news bulletin can signify its acceptance into standard English.

That's some responsibility.

The English Speaking Board, set up by the distinguished academic, Sir Michael Dummett, does not believe the corporation is taking it seriously enough. The Board, which includes such notables as Lord Tebbit, wrote to the BBC to tell them they were not happy. The BBC replied that it was not its job 'to preserve any specific form of the English language but to reflect its fluid and ever-changing nature'.

The Board dismissed this as 'neutral'. It argued that the BBC could not evade the fact that it was an 'active participant in, and not a mute observer of, the process of linguistic development'. It wants the BBC to appoint a language adviser, supported by a network of unpaid monitors. I'm not quite sure what the adviser or the monitors would do. I spent five minutes on the phone with Lord Tebbit and we agreed what the problems were: too many hackneyed phrases; too much inflated language; too much poor grammar; too many slang expressions passing themselves off as modern usage. So that's me dealt with. I promised him that I shall try harder in future.

I'm only half joking. Yes, I am guilty of all that (and worse) from time to time – though Lord Tebbit was gracious enough to accept that one does not expect the same precision in spontaneous conversation as one would expect from a scripted piece. But the point is that I am conscious of it when I do it, and I can't quite see how it would help to have an adviser or a team of monitors drawing my attention to my solecisms and my hackneyed phrases.

In any case, the monitors already exist. I picture them sitting at kitchen tables across the nation, radios in front of them and notepads beside them, waiting for us poor souls to fall into some linguistic trap. The letters arrive a few days later. One of the things they tell you is that people care passionately about pronunciation.

Hard or Soft?

These days the BBC is terribly sensitive to accusations of class or regional bias. It was not always so. If you appeared on the wireless in the old days you spoke posh. Just about the only regional or working-class accents you ever heard were in drama or comedy. Announcers, newsreaders and presenters of programmes were middle-class and Home Counties types – all sounding as if they had been to a minor public school and knew the rule about whether milk should be poured into the bone china cup before or after the tea. (It's after, I think.) There was special dispensation for 'characters', such as Wilfred Pickles who was allowed to amuse us with his quaint northern accent, but that was about it.

Nobody, so far as I know, ever told you to speak posh but that was probably because there was no need to. It was simply taken for granted. It seeped up through the floorboards. I remember poking fun at Sue MacGregor when a clip of her presenting *Woman's Hour* in the sixties was played in some archive programme. She spent her childhood in South Africa and I asked her how she had come to sound like a combination of the Queen Mother and an elocution teacher from Surrey.

'Ha!' she said. 'Have you listened to recordings of yourself from those days?' And she was right. I

was born in a district of Cardiff called Splott, where
a was so hard you could smash concrete with it.
Splott people made Scouse sound like Surrey. They
were as likely to have milk jugs in the kitchen as a
Rembrandt in the outdoor lavatory: the milk came
straight from the bottle. I was, as the saying had it
back then, as common as muck. But you'd never
have guessed it from the way I spoke when I started
appearing on the BBC. Not that I always got it
right.

One perceptive writer in *The Times* noticed my
difficulty with pronouncing 'Pakistan': it never came
out the same way twice. Sometimes the first *a* would
be hard, as in cat, and the second one soft, as in
calm; the next time it would be vice versa. Sometimes both were hard and at others both were soft.
I think he worked out the number of possible vari-
ations but I'd prefer not to remember. My pronunciation was a combination of Splott and posh –
Splosh, perhaps. I was a tortured soul.

It's only in the last few years that I have had the
confidence to revert to type and accept that I shall
always be a hard *a* man. And nobody minds. On
the contrary, there is a special welcome for those
who do not speak with what was once called
'received pronunciation'. The refined Home Counties delivery has more or less vanished from the
airwaves. My own role in that revolution was small

compared with a man whose accent turned him into a national icon.

Why No Brum?

My boss called me in one day and asked me to put the new man through his paces in the studio. That was when I first met John Cole. I spent a couple of hours with him, showing him how an autocue worked and listening to him deliver his lines. I went back to my boss and reported, with deep sadness, that John might be a brilliant newspaper journalist but would never make it as a broadcaster outside Northern Ireland. Nobody would understand a word he said. Fortunately, they took no notice of me, and John and his hideous overcoat went on to broadcasting glory.

Radio Four still has some of the old school – Peter Donaldson, Harriet Cass, Charlotte Green – and fine broadcasters they are. But they are becoming the exception rather than the rule. The new people, like Jim Leigh and Carolyn Brown with their flat northern vowels, are as far removed from the old Home Service as Greg Dyke was from Lord Reith. Most regional accents are now acceptable – or even welcomed – though some are, curiously, still more welcome than others.

Why do we seldom hear a real Birmingham

accent? Sue Lawley spoke Brum as a child, but abandoned it pretty smartly when she grew up. Estuary English seems to be compulsory on children's programmes and anywhere pop music is played, but still largely frowned upon on Radio Four. Good. I don't like glottal stops (especially when they are adopted by public-school-educated politicians because they think it makes them sound cool) and I don't like people saying 'fink' unless they have a speech impediment.

Pronunciation is still a live topic in the BBC. Half the audience gets cross if we pronounce 'controversy' with the emphasis on 'con' and the other half if we emphasise 'trov'. I'm a 'con' man myself, for what it's worth. To judge by my mailbag, the audience is united in loathing American pronunciations: 'research' and 'romance', for instance, with the emphasis on the first syllable. I'm with them on that. Horrible.

We argue endlessly about which words should be anglicised and why. We'd never dream of saying 'Paree' or 'Roma' so why are the poor old newsreaders on Radio Four flogged if they fail to pronounce other foreign place names exactly as the locals do it? It baffles me. Sometimes they are given the wrong advice and by the time we get it right the whole nation is getting it wrong. We started saying 'Al Kie-eeda' and it stuck. But no Arabic speaker would dream of pronouncing it that way: there's no 'ee' in the middle. But it's too late now. It probably doesn't matter. It's just profoundly irritating if, by some fluke, you happen to know the right way to say it.

What does matter is when people who should know better can't be bothered to find out how to pronounce the names of places in this country. I speak as a Welshman, you understand. I do not expect your typical Englishman to get Ynysybwl exactly right but I do expect professional BBC broadcasters to know how to pronounce the name of my country which, in Welsh, is Cymru. Even political correspondents, who have to deal with only half a dozen parties, frequently mispronounce Plaid Cymru. They actually make it more difficult than it is. In Welsh the letter *y* almost always becomes *u*, and the *u* becomes ee, so Cymru is pronounced 'Kumree', not some tortured version of Koomroo. It takes a second to learn it and it's sheer laziness not to make the effort. End of rant.

A Matter of Style

The battle of pronunciation will never be won or lost – although it's really more a light skirmish than a fight to the death. What matters more than how we speak is what we say. And there are plenty of letters about that, too. Some list the clichés they say are used most often:

- grinds to a halt
- at the end of the day
- on the back burner
- on the ground
- on the back foot
- on hold
- up for grabs
- moment of truth
- a question mark hangs over
- conspicuous by its absence
- hail of bullets
- shrouded in mystery
- calm before the storm
- explore every avenue
- leave no stone unturned

Tensions invariably run high and so do emotions. One day I'm going to say emotions run low just to see if anyone notices. Feuds usually simmer, but I did hear a colleague announcing with great confidence that one particular feud was 'simmering even more fiercely'. Peace talks are aimed at resolving any given crisis. I suppose if they weren't they would not be peace talks. On the subject of violence we usually find that gunmen have shot someone – as opposed to knifing them.

Most of these have been used by generations of journalists. Orwell called them 'silly words and expressions', but he was hopelessly unrealistic about our readiness to stop using them. Fifty years ago he referred to two which, he said, had been 'killed by the jeers of a few journalists'. What were they? 'Explore every avenue' and 'leave no stone un-turned'. Which goes to show that even a genius can get it wrong.

Journalists invent verbal constructions that no one in the real world ever uses. We endow days of the week with the power of vision. How else to explain that 'Tomorrow sees the publication of the (invariably long-awaited) report'? The BBC, like newspapers, loves words such as

- axe (as in jobs)
- quit (as in resign)
- oust (as in force out)
- bid (instead of attempt)
- blow (disappointment)
- probe (inquiry)

Newspapers use 'set to' instead of 'likely to' and so do we. In a newspaper a dispute becomes a 'clash' and we follow suit.

There is a perfectly good reason for the papers to do this sort of thing: you need short words for headlines. I can think of no reason at all to use them in broadcast English. Our constraint is time, not space. It saves precisely one ninth of a second to use a one-syllable word instead of a three-syllable word and even the *Today* programme at its most packed does not measure time in fractions of a second – not even when we demand that our interviewee summarise the prospects for the European economy and the causes of the First World War in the fifteen seconds before the pips sound.

Something else we copy from newspapers is the use of the present tense for headlines as in:

- A grandmother is jailed for refusing to pay council tax.
- Three people are killed in a motorway pile-up.

This is nonsense. They are not being jailed or killed as we speak. I suppose we do this sort of thing because we think it makes the event sound more dramatic. It doesn't. It just makes us sound silly and out of touch with our viewers and listeners. So does the use of journalese in general. In real life people do not talk of 'blunders' but of mistakes. They do not say the 'death toll was seven': they say 'Seven people died.' They almost never use 'eleventh hour'; we use it often. They seldom say that someone is 'fighting for his life' when they know the poor chap is unconscious and being kept alive by a machine.

We use arcane as well as hackneyed language. As

I write, my radio tells me that a reporter in Baghdad 'witnessed' a terrible bomb explosion in which many people died. As it happens, I had spoken to the reporter a few hours earlier and he had told me in graphic language that he had been within yards of the explosion and was lucky to be alive. So why 'witnessed'? It is the careful, legalistic language of the court room dragged into the dangerous streets of a city at war with itself and it is entirely inappropriate.

No one outside newspaper headlines and broadcasting newsrooms says 'amid' and 'vowed to', and when did you last 'pledge' something? Probably when you got married. Nor do people say someone 'sustained fatal injuries'. They say, 'He was killed.'

... And Now the Weather Forecast

Ah, yes, the weather forecast. If complaining about the weather is our favourite national pastime, complaining about the forecast is pretty popular too. They never get it right, do they? Well, actually, they do – almost all the time. We tend to remember only when they get it wrong. And here's another thing: we don't listen to the forecasts. We hear them, but we don't listen. I suspect that is not entirely our fault. There is something about the way the forecast is delivered on radio which means that by the time it's finished most of us have no idea what was said. Yes, there's going to be snow in Scotland, but will the rain spreading from the east affect us in the west or was it the Midlands that will get wet, and will the showers peter out or won't they?

This has puzzled me for years. I was beginning to think it was just my own inability to concentrate, so I was rather relieved when Charles Moore, the former editor of the *Daily Telegraph*, confirmed my suspicion. He wrote in the *Spectator* that, as a countryman, he took a keen interest in what the weather was doing – especially at weekends. But he never found out because, by the time the forecast had finished, his attention had drifted away. So why should this be?

It's not as if all the forecasters follow rigidly the same formula. None of them comes into the studio with a script of what to say. Some bring in little maps, some a few notes on a pad and some only a stopwatch. It was always unnerving to watch David Braine deliver his forecast. He would sit there, stop-watch in one hand and nothing in the other, stare at the desk in front of him and deliver his words faultlessly, for all the world as though he were reading a prepared script laid out on the desk and only he could see it. Quite spooky, really. We kept waiting for him to fumble or simply forget, but he never did.

The BBC's forecasters are the best in the business – all of them trained meteorologists, underpaid and forced to work rotten hours. I know one who moonlights as a gardener to earn a bit of extra cash: ten pounds an hour, if you're interested. This is not the glamorous job it's cracked up to be. Nor is it an easy one. Bizarrely, they have more or less the same air time to fill whether there are clear blue skies over the entire northern hemisphere and only one word is needed ('hot') or whether their charts look like something a spaced-out monkey created with a limitless supply of ink. That's the sort of day Michael Fish (now retired) had in mind when he said, 'There's an awful lot of weather about today.' Perhaps that's the sort of language one listener had in mind when she wrote to me with this observation:

> TV and radio weather forecasting has a quixotic branch of English all its own.

I tend to agree with that but I need to be a little careful here. I seem to have alienated half the listeners to *Today* by refusing to join in the national celebrations when the sun shines for more than an hour or two at a time. I like the sun – but I also like rain. What baffles me is the language forecasters use after weeks of blistering sun (not a regular occurrence, I grant you) have shrivelled every last leaf and our parks look like the Gobi Desert. The rivers have run dry and the bleached bones of dead livestock glint in the sun. And what do they say when the 'glorious' weather finally looks as though it may break? 'There is a threat of rain.'

Yes, a 'threat'. Why is rain always a threat and sun always a promise? Don't they know that rain is what makes this such a delightful country in which to live? Don't they know that without rain we would all be dead? Yes, of course they do, but they also know what an absurd attitude we have towards weather in this country and they have been browbeaten or intimidated into accepting the notion that dry is good and wet is bad. Bonkers, but there we are.

Who's Organising the Rain?

The forecasts are full of little linguistic mysteries. I have been lectured on air by several forecasters for failing, for instance, to understand the difference between showers and rain. What if the shower lasts a long time? When does it stop being a shower and become rain? And what, in the name of sanity, is 'organised rain'? Some of the language is inspired.

'Today's highs will be a little lower.'

That cannot have come about by accident; someone

deserves an award for it. I also like 'outbreaks of rain and fresh sunshine'. I'm even prepared to tolerate 'spits and spots' of rain, though it seems to irritate everyone else. It may not be technically faultless but you get a pretty good idea of what to expect.

For one listener, Derrick White, the killer is the misuse and overuse of 'murky'. He claims they cannot say 'misty' without extending it to 'misty and murky'. He wrote this to me one January after a forecaster said the evening would be 'misty and murky':

Of course it will be bloody murky! January evenings are totally murky. It has to do with the absence of sun, which occurs at about five o'clock.

A little intemperate, maybe, but you cannot fault his logic.

The jargon irritates many listeners: 'dry scenario' and 'wind-chill factor' or even 'temperature-wise'. Another irritation is the reluctance of some forecasters to use main verbs, 'In Scotland, rain moving across . . .' and their love of the dangling clause, 'Turning to the north, the clouds will thicken . . .' but we are all guilty of that sort of thing.

I suspect the real problem is that forecasters, like most broadcasters, are told to keep it cheerful, use the vernacular wherever possible and make it matey. Thus we get:

> 'We're going to be talking snow over the next few days.'

And

> 'We're looking at gales across southern England.'

The problem with that is it makes the forecaster sound like a plumber giving you an estimate you would much rather not hear. 'Sorry, squire, we're looking at a new boiler here and then there's . . .'

Ingratiate . . . Irritate

This linguistic virus is contagious and I fear none of us is immune. It is at its most virulent in children's television.

I do not expect presenters on programmes aimed at teenagers to speak like the Lord Chamberlain addressing the Queen, but I'm not sure they have to be quite so ingratiating and strive quite so frantic-ally to be seen to have street-cred.

The virus has spread even into the offices of those inventive folk who create the promotional trails for Radio Four. Do we really need to hear this sort of language, from a cricketer, used in a trail for that most staid and easy-going of programmes – redolent of lazy summer afternoons, the thwack of leather on willow – *Test Match Special*?

'I NEED to win! I NEED to take a wicket!'

The language of fierce, aggressive individualism seems at odds with a team game like cricket. It would have been unthinkable a generation ago and it should be unthinkable today. The language of hard-sell marketing aimed at blokes with cans of lager in their hands isn't what the BBC should be using to get people to listen to their cricket commentary. After all, when they tune in what they'll get (thankfully) is still something closer to the poetry of John Arlott or the comedy of Brian Johnston than to the relentless drone of Murray Walker backed by a chorus of wailing cars. Maybe they have another game at the back of their minds. As someone wrote to me gleefully to complain:

'The cricket season kicks off this week.'

Who'd Adjudicate?

Since we are guilty of all these things, why should the BBC not follow the advice of the English Speaking Board and appoint an adviser? Two questions have to be asked. The first is, who should get the job?

Perhaps you would like it. You probably think you speak and write perfectly good English. Or maybe it should go to a distinguished academic who has spent most of his life studying language. He will know the rules and he will be able to apply the correct standard. But that takes us to the second big question.

What 'standard' might that be? Yours or mine? Or that of the teenager next door with the drug habit or the old bloke down the pub who still uses slang from the fifties? Those two might inhabit a different universe, let alone speak a different language, but you could argue that they are equally entitled to have their language respected. And how is the adviser going to arbitrate on what changes are acceptable and what are not?

I referred earlier to my dislike of the word 'outwith' – not least because I am never quite sure what it means. Neither, I'm sure, does at least half the audience understand it. But when I fulminate against it, I am met by the younger members of the *Today* team (they are *all* younger than me) with patronising smiles and that infuriating 'Calm down, Granddad, times move on and *we* all know what it means' expression.

Vocabulary is a tricky area – but not as tricky as grammar. I may not worry too much about prepositions but I loathe split infinitives. No adviser will change my view on that and nor, I suspect, would he change yours, whatever it may be. So, critical though I am of much of our output, I think the BBC is right when it says it is not part of its role to preserve any specific form of the language, but reflect its changing nature. Something it could do is publish its style guide and then pay close attention to the row that will, inevitably, follow.

A Matter of Style

Almost all news organisations have their own style guides and most update them regularly. The *Manchester Guardian*'s style guide of 1928 was greatly concerned that its journalists should know how to describe one's servants. The cook general had no hyphen but the house parlour-maid and the between-maid did. As a matter of style, 'gent' was never to be used – except in advertisements. Spelling was important, though today's *Guardian* writers have relatively little need of the guidance offered on 'postilion' and 'sepoy' and I can't quite remember the last time a 'guttapercha' appeared in the *Guardian*'s columns. It's a tree found on the Malaysian peninsula, since you ask. Mineral oils are always sold per ton, whereas olive oils and fish oils are sold per tun. But you probably knew that.

The most recent *Guardian* guide includes the words 'berks' and 'wankers'. I don't *think* they were in the 1928 guide. Lest you fret about the distinction, the *Guardian* offers the thoughts of Kingsley Amis:

> Berks are careless, coarse, crass, gross and of what anybody would agree is a lower social class than one's own; wankers are prissy, fussy, priggish, prim and of what they would probably misrepresent as a higher social class than one's own.

Magnificent.

The BBC style guide lacks such helpful advice, but is otherwise remarkably sensible. It recognises that you cannot please all the listeners all the time, hence the advice to tread the fine line between conservatism and radicalism. And there are some splendid examples of how sentences can go wrong:

> For the second time in six months, a prisoner at Durham jail has died after hanging himself in his cell.

It is, apparently, not only prisoners in Durham who have the ability to die more than once:

> A suicide bomber has struck again in Jerusalem.

Nor is society safe once the wicked have departed:

> Sixty women have come forward to claim they have been assaulted by a dead gynaecologist.

And still on the subject of death:

> It's a sad and tragic fact that if you're a farmer you are three times more likely to die than the average factory worker.

I wonder if it's too late to get a job in a factory – though presumably even factory workers die eventually.

The best advice when you're on the radio or television, as the guide recognises, is to keep it simple: subject-verb-object. That's not because the audience is too thick to follow complicated thoughts but because listening is different from reading – especially listening to the radio when it has to compete with the kids fighting, the cat being sick behind the sofa and all the other crises of domestic life.

Complicated sentences are risky. If the listeners don't get the point when it is made, they can't spool back or refer to the previous sentence. Too many subordinate clauses set up barriers to understanding. Here's a nice example of that:

> With what his political opponents called a leap in the dark, the Prime Minister today committed Britain to a European daylight-saving regime.

The problem with that sentence is that by the time you have worked out roughly what it means it's too late: another three sentences have come and gone. So, unless you are a very dedicated listener indeed and concentrating terribly hard, you will probably give up.

The other curious thing about the sentence is the placing of 'today'. If I ask a political correspondent in an unscripted interview about the timing of an announcement by the Prime Minister he will probably say, 'The Prime Minister is going to make the announcement today.' Yet when that modest piece of information has passed through the machine, is written down and delivered by the newsreader it will invariably come out like this:

> 'The Prime Minister will today announce . . .'

This baffles me. It forces the newsreader to insert unseen commas around 'today' and breaks the flow of the sentence. I know there are bigger things in this world to worry about but it is profoundly irritating – and I have never been able to find anyone to explain why it happens.

Nor do I know why we say 'later' today when we are talking about something that will happen in a few hours' time or 'Earlier I asked him . . .'. It is bound to be 'later' if it has yet to happen and it is bound to be 'earlier' if it has already happened. Small things, I know, but they all add up. Writing for radio is a tricky business if we hope to keep the attention of the audience. So it is with television.

Seeing and Hearing

Writing commentaries for pictures can be tricky. How much should a reporter say when you can see the pictures for yourself? The answer, I think, is as little as possible. In this business, less is usually more. Martin Bell, the finest television reporter of his generation, was the master of talking over the pictures. He did it by never writing anything down.

Most of us lesser mortals would look at the pictures on the machine in the editing suite, tell the picture editor what we wanted, take notes of how long each shot was, go away and write our script.

Then we would record it over the pictures. Not Martin. He would look at the pictures, decide on a shot and ask the editor how long it was. Then he would amble out of the editing suite and mutter to himself. When he came back he would use a 'lip' microphone and speak the words over the pictures.

I doubt that his 'scripts' would stand up under strict grammatical scrutiny and the sentences probably broke every rule in the book, but they did superbly what they were meant to do: they helped the viewer understand what they were watching. Or, in Martin's words, they 'caressed' the pictures. I have known better writers in television news than Martin. I have never known anyone use language more effectively to complement the pictures.

Our Responsibility

So we journalists are no better and no worse than everyone else who uses the common language. We mangle with the best of them. But we have a particular responsibility and we should not be allowed to get away with it. It's important that viewers and listeners give us a hard time. There should be a permanent row about usage. Keep stoking it.

CHAPTER TWELVE

Who Are They Kidding?

Schoolboys in ancient Greece had a more limited curriculum than children have today: no computer studies for a start, and I doubt that their teachers taught them about safe sex by rolling condoms on to bananas. But they did learn rhetoric. We have a pretty sniffy attitude towards it these days. We scarcely use the word and when we do it is almost always coupled with the pejorative 'windy' – which shows how little we have learned in the past couple of thousand years. Rhetoric is about using language to influence and manipulate.

The most inflammatory rhetoric in the hands of a great orator can be the ultimate weapon of mass destruction. Look at Hitler in his prime, whipping the German people into a frenzy. Or Churchill, using his slightly more measured tones to inspire a threatened nation by promising nothing but blood, toil, tears and sweat. The rhetoric the ancients learned includes the great skill of covering up what you're really saying but getting the message across none the less. It accommodates that precious thing politicians crave: deniability. When Marc Antony said he had come 'to bury Caesar, not to praise him' the crowd needed to keep its wits about it to see what he was up to.

The language of good old-fashioned rhetoric links thought to argument. Even a highly rhetorical speech should give us something to think about and, perhaps, object to. It should convince the listener through the clever use of language. It is about words as weapons: not the bunker-buster that blasts everything into dust, but the cruise missile that turns left at the traffic-lights and slips down a chimney, unnoticed until it explodes. Good rhetoric is subtle as well as seductive. It is what we mostly lack today.

We have moved from the skilful rhetoric of ancient Greece and wartime Britain to the language of the marketing men. They too use language to manipulate, but it has nothing to do with argument. Words are used – if they are used at all – to conjure up moods, images and subconscious associations in order to sell. The intention is not to persuade us through convincing argument, or even to appeal to our passions. It is to subvert our emotions so that we submit to the message, only half aware that we have done so. And it works – which is why the politicians have adopted some of the techniques.

Affordable?

The pioneers in this field were advertising and public-relations executives. Argument is not something that interests them very much. The rudimentary stuff has been going on for years, but presumably it still works or they would have dumped it. We are told that the mobile phone costs 'only' £9.99 because £10 sounds so much more. If we buy a shirt in a sale we are told we can 'save' a tenner. If we want oranges in a supermarket we can take two bags and 'get one free'. We know that none of these statements is true, but this sort of stuff is now so familiar we take it for granted. We are being manipulated, but so what?

Still, it's worth keeping an eye open for new ones. 'Affordable' has crept in. This is a great marketing word – mostly because it is devoid of any meaning whatsoever. Affordable to whom? To everybody? That is manifestly nonsense. I saw 'affordable' flats advertised. The prices 'started at' £199,000. In Knightsbridge that is obviously inexpensive; walls and floors would be optional extras. But many people, equally obviously, could not have afforded them.

Modern advertisers – or many of them – scoff at the notion that advertisements should convey information. That's not what it's about at all. The purpose is to create 'positive' associations with a product. Hence the sponsorship deals with famous sportsmen that leave them rich enough to buy one of those £199,000 flats every week if the fancy takes them.

A lot of television and cinema advertising – especially cinema – now uses no language at all. It is not even stated explicitly what links the products with the mini films advertising them. The art of using language to persuade has given way to an entirely different skill: combining visual images of beautiful young people doing highly improbable things together in a very sexy way. Words, which give rise to argument, or at least an element of thought, have given way to images which are passively absorbed.

Brand New

Straightforward advertising is only the start of it. The new thing is 'branding' – not that the concept itself is new, just the approach. These days, brand is all.

When a BBC channel controller was asked how she proposed to improve the audience figures for a particularly lacklustre evening she said we 'need to construct a new story ... maybe move some better-known brands'. I wonder when they stopped calling them programmes. Still, I suppose it's better than 'product', which is how programmes are also described by certain television executives who would be just as happy selling baked beans.

Products have always been given names that have nothing to do with what they are. Sometimes the brand is so successful that the new name replaces the process for which it was designed – which is why we Hoover carpets rather than vacuum them.

It sometimes works the other way. Horlicks has entered the vocabulary, but I bet the smarty-pants who came up with the name never imagined a future British foreign secretary using it to describe a dodgy dossier intended to make the case for taking us to war against Iraq. But, then, few people used the rude word it rhymes with in those more innocent days.

Coca-Cola is said to be the world's most famous brand. Their British company wanted us to buy bottled water from them. So they tried to get a slice of the business and the name they came up with for their water was Dasani. No, I have no idea what it means either. It doesn't seem to appear in any foreign dictionary. But the 'branding consultants' who created it claimed the word would suggest 'relaxation, pureness and replenishment'.

This sort of guff takes language about as far as it can get from thought and from expressing anything of substance. You can almost forgive the barmy name; what hurts is the absurd pretensions they attach to it.

It flopped – in a big way. There were a couple of problems. The first was that the newspapers reported with great glee that the water did not come from some mountain spring, filtered through ancient peat and bottled at source. It came from the tap and got mucked about with – or 'treated', as the company put it. That was bad enough. The killer blow was that the mucking-about process left the water with high levels of something unpleasant called bromate. So the water was withdrawn from the supermarket shelves. There was scarcely a dry eye in the house.

Hokum Words

You can understand why a new product needs a new name – it has to be called something, however silly – but why 'rebrand' old, established companies? Sometimes it happens because a company has got into such a mess the bosses think the only way to rescue it is to persuade us that it's a different company.

Often it's for no better reason than that the consultants who specialise in this sort of thing have managed to persuade the bosses it would be a good idea. Lord knows what made the Royal Mail change its name to Consignia. How many years has the Royal Mail been in business? A three-year-old could have told them that we were hardly likely to go around after all this time using the silly new word. 'Morning, love, has the Consignia man been yet?' But they did it and it cost a fortune and, sure enough, they were forced to change it back and that cost another fortune.

The international mailing company TNT are not quite as old as the Royal Mail but they're very successful. Yet they changed their name too. They started calling themselves Spring. Again, why? No doubt the branding experts reckoned we would be seduced by associations with the word: a 'spring in the step' or 'the new shoots of spring' or some such tosh.

My suspicion is that the consultants have developed their own language to bamboozle their clients. Andersen Consulting decided to change its name to accenture. The word, it goes without saying, is pure hokum. The lower-case initial letter has become very trendy, so that explains that. And the funny little accent we've never seen anywhere else suggests they are so clever they know things we haven't yet caught up with. When it stops being trendy they'll probably have to change it to something else, which means more fees for someone. As

to what this strange new creature does, here is part
of the explanation from its website:

> Accenture is committed to uncovering the key
> ingredients to help our clients . . .

There's a hint here: cooking. Or perhaps not,
because they go on to say they are 'committed to
delivering innovation'. Here we are again, back to
the dreary notion of delivering things. I hope they
have a good 'customer service' department. 'I'd like
to complain because that innovation delivery was
supposed to arrive yesterday and it's still not here.
It's a damned nuisance, there's always a big demand
for innovations at this time of year and if you can't
deliver we'll have to go elsewhere.'

The emptiness of meaning in this sort of manipulative use of words often stares everyone in the face
except the bright boys who come up with them.
When four train-operating companies in East
Anglia decided to merge their operations, they had
to find a name for their new company. They came
up with One. You can imagine the young branding
consultants banging on about the theme of unity
and 'one-ness' and how everyone would feel so good
about it. What they probably did not think about
was the poor sod standing on the platform on a
cold December morning straining to hear the

announcement from the muffled Tannoy when his train is late yet again:

> 'The 7.20 One service to Norwich will now arrive on platform two. The 8.20 One service has also been delayed and will arrive at 8.31 on platform one.'

Company directors have always been susceptible to smooth-talking consultants and market-speak. Sadly, they are not alone. Even distinguished musicians succumb. The Lindsay String Quartet, renowned throughout the world, decided that henceforth they wished to be known simply as The Lindsays. What on earth is gained by removing the very information that tells people what you are? The new name made them sound like a low-budget American soap opera imported to fill a backwater slot in daytime television when what they really do is play late Beethoven sublimely. This is truly a mystery.

Who Are We Dealing With?

The invented names of today do more than try our patience with their fatuity. They create a façade behind which everything becomes obscure. Language is used to make things opaque rather than transparent. These new branded names, which have no meaning and are conjured up by putting together syllables that sound attractive or have some bogus connection with what will subliminally appeal to us, tell us nothing either of the people behind the image or of what their company gets up to. The smile is there to conceal.

When companies were called by the names of the people who owned them – there really was a Mr W. H. Smith, a bookseller who had sons – at least you had the sense of human beings at the heart of the business even if it wasn't possible to ring them up and speak to them. But now it feels very different, and the new bogus names convey the difference.

It's as though big corporations, for all their talk about the vital need to communicate, want to do the opposite. We cannot even talk to their employees. Computers write us letters and answering-machines tell us which buttons to press. If we do eventually reach a human being she is probably in Bangalore – hugely over-qualified to be answering our humdrum enquiries and, anyway, herself reduced by the rules to formulaic responses. She may, poor soul, have to endure regular briefing on the latest goings-on in Albert Square to be able to put us at our ease, but the corporate distance remains intact.

The Abbey National Bank went one further with

its rebranding. It did not merely change its name (I suppose calling it 'abbey' really does make all the difference) but it did something funny with the logo. The letters shuffle erratically above an imaginary line and their edges fade off into an infinite fuzz. It conveys the impression of receding into the distance. Not, perhaps, ideal for a bank holding your money, but there you are.

What it's probably meant to do is suggest gentleness rather than a hard edge – none of this nasty corporate tough talk. The words on its website support that impression. This sort of thing:

> Last year we *relaunched* our business with the aim of turning banking on its head. We asked you for suggestions about how we could do this and you certainly gave us plenty to think about. See what you had to say *here*.
>
> We've been really busy recently and we're not slowing down. We've loads of great ideas to help you get on top of your finances. For example, a *Bright Future Gift* is the perfect way to give money, whatever the occasion.
>
> Now we're in a new tax year, it's a great time to take stock of your finances and make sure you're making the most of your money. Though we realise that there are at least a million things more interesting than sorting out your savings, take a look at

Abbey's simple tax-efficient *savings* and *invest-ments* options, and take full advantage of your per-sonal tax-free allowance. Or pop in to have a chat at your *nearest branch* and find out more.

And while we're on the subject of sorting out your finances, remember that our *loans* are really affordable and you can use them for anything you want.

You finish reading that and half expect the door to burst open, and the beaming face of abbey's chair-man, Lord Burns, to pop round it, saying, 'Hi! I'm Terry! Here's a fiver!'

I do not want big business to be my close buddy, taking me off down the pub and telling me they'll always be 'there for me', any more than I want them to be remote-controlled juggernauts comman-deering the language to manipulate me. I want to have a straightforward and slightly formal relation-ship and I want a straightforward and slightly for-mal language to be used between us. A degree of formality is needed to protect the space within which we can be sceptical and critical.

Just Keep Smiling

When business and all its corporate imitators are not talking the mind-numbing management-speak we shed tears over earlier, they are talking the evangelical puff-speak of PR. You catch it in the absurd mottoes, or mini mission statements, that now seem to be the obligatory badges of corporate identity.

Unilever gave itself a new, friendly-seeming logo early in 2004. The message it wanted to convey was that it aims 'to add vitality to life – help people to feel good, look good and get more out of life'. The pharmaceutical firm GlaxoSmithKline announces, alongside its name, on its website that 'Our global quest is to improve the quality of life by enabling people to do more, feel better and live longer.' We can, no doubt, thank Hollywood for 'quest'. It conjures up the image of the mythic knight roaming the world in search of the Holy Grail. This, incidentally, from the company facing lawsuits in New York for allegedly withholding research suggesting that in some tests its anti-depressants led children to attempt suicide.

It is not only commercial interests that play this game. The Department for Education and Skills offers this contribution:

creating opportunity, releasing potential, achieving excellence.

How very reassuring. You might like to know, too, that Scotland Yard is 'working for a safer London'. And there were you thinking it wanted our streets filled with muggers and rapists. A sixth-form college sells itself as 'a passport to opportunity'. It cannot be long before the Church of England joins in. Something like 'Working together towards an after-life for all'.

My own *Today* programme must not be left out. I suggest something like:

Arguing and interrupting . . . for a better *Today*!

PR language uses words to create effect and not to convey meaning. Try the test I suggested earlier in the book and insert a negative:

The Department for Education does *not* want to create opportunity . . .

This is worse than management-speak. This stuff is insidious. As the satirist Armando Iannucci has pointed out, in its way it's as Orwellian as *Newspeak*:

This new dictionary of upbeat, light-headed, fresh-faced optimism imposes a fiction on thought, to manufacture a world view from which it's increasingly difficult to diverge.

If you get a parking ticket in the London borough of Camden and want to challenge it, you will find yourself having to communicate with an office called 'Camden Parking Solutions'. A solution to your problem is, of course, precisely what is not on offer. They want you to pay up and shut up. Why not be honest about it?

This ghastly language that admits only upbeat words can probably be traced back to the America of the 1950s, the era of 'positive affirmation' and huge bestsellers like Norman Vincent Peale's *The Power of Positive Thinking*. The message was: if you tell yourself you can do something, you can do it; saying is everything. Words feed the will. For this to work, only half the vocabulary can be allowed – only words to do with determination, work, confidence, success. Words that reflect the other side of the human condition – frailty, error and so on – are airbrushed out. The puff-speak of the PR world tries to bamboozle us with the same technique. It hopes that if it bangs on for long enough in this half-language it will manipulate us into seeing the world as it wants us to. We should not co-operate.

CHAPTER THIRTEEN

Can Words Change the World?

You are on the London Underground, going home after a hard day at the office, jammed upright by a dozen sweaty bodies and thoroughly fed up. You spot this advertisement:

> Some people think that being tired is just part of today's hectic lifestyle. But being tired even after a good night's sleep, or feeling that you just want to nod-off when you are travelling to and from work, can be signs of daily fatigue.

A number of thoughts may occur to you. If you are a stickler for grammar there will be mild irritation at the bad English – three errors in only two sentences – but it's the final phrase that may stick in your mind: 'daily fatigue'. Of course! That's what you've got! A condition known as daily fatigue. It's just like any other illness – flu or lumbago or asthma. And you thought you were just knackered after a lousy day at work, not enough sleep and too much to drink the night before. You are a sufferer from a condition or, better still, a victim of that condition. What matters now is to get help.

No problem:

Take one capsule every day for a month and help say goodbye to daily fatigue.

The capsules may indeed provide a bit of a pick-me-up – probably not as much as a good night's sleep, a little less booze, a walk in the fresh air and a banana or two – and they will almost certainly do no harm. The harm has already been done with the creation of a condition called 'daily fatigue'.

There is – or so my doctor tells me – no such thing. If you are permanently tired there will be an underlying reason for it and no amount of capsule-popping will cure it. Cocaine might be effective but it becomes expensive after a while and it is not recommended by your average family doctor.

Occasional tiredness is something from which everyone who has ever lived has 'suffered' – with the possible exception of Margaret Thatcher. To describe it as a condition is a linguistic trick. It turns a subjective experience into an objective thing. Persuade us that we suffer from that condition and you may then be able to persuade us that we need the 'cure' on offer. It is manipulative.

Of course there have always been snake-oil sales-men. I vaguely remember that Carter's Liver Pills cured all known ills – or did they just cure your liver? Even good old Horlicks made some pretty daft claims years ago. It cured us of 'night starvation', as I recall. I don't suppose anyone really believed such a condition existed, but it was a shade more exciting than telling us what we already knew: a warm milky drink before you went to bed might help you sleep – even if the powder in it did taste foul.

The more outrageous claims have been knocked on the head by the new laws. It is illegal to promise us that we will live for ever if we keep taking a company's tablets. We wouldn't believe it anyway. We know you can't cure cancer with a pill. But this new use of words is tougher to crack and more insidious. It manipulates us by creating terms that change the way we look at things. It takes something that may be extremely complex, removes the com-plexity, and produces a nice neat phrase or 'con-dition' that we can all understand.

Trust Me: I'm an Expert

Doctors say patients would prefer to know what is wrong with them even if the diagnosis is pretty terrible: it is the uncertainty we find most distressing. Mostly they oblige. A broken leg is, when all's said and done, a broken leg. It gets more difficult when the symptoms are less obvious.

The distinction between mental illness and mental well-being can sometimes be a bit fuzzy. Is the person behaving a bit oddly because he is, well, a bit odd or because there's something wrong with him? Has he 'got' something? This takes us into the strange world of 'syndromes' – the new vogue word in health matters. Syndromes are not like viruses: they cannot be seen under a microscope and their existence cannot be objectively proven. It is a matter of decision, not discovery. The experts in the field must decide whether a particular symptom – or set of symptoms – arises often enough for a 'new' syndrome to be announced to the world. This gives them great power. We adopt their language, then see the world in terms of it. That is one effect. The other is that it may affect how the world sees us – sometimes with disastrous results.

Munchausen's Syndrome by Proxy is a relatively new syndrome. Those who 'suffer' from it may, it is claimed, draw attention to themselves by harming those closest to them. I am obviously not qualified to say whether or not it exists; there is a fierce debate about it among the experts. But I do know something about the terrible consequences of getting it wrong.

Innocent 'Sufferers'

One of the most harrowing mornings of my life was spent interviewing Angela and Terry Cannings, who had one daughter and three sons. All three boys died soon after they were born. It is hard to conceive of a greater tragedy – but there was indeed worse to come. Mrs Cannings was convicted of murdering her children and sent to jail. You can imagine how she was treated by the other prisoners. A child murderer is the most loathed of all.

Mrs Cannings was set free when the appeal court ruled that she was innocent. She was not – and never had been – afflicted by Munchausen's. She was a victim not of a syndrome but of the experts' willingness to believe in their own creation: something to which they had given a name.

Attention Deficit Hyperactivity Disorder (ADHD) is another relatively new syndrome. When it was first 'identified' in 1991 a thousand children were diagnosed with it. Ten years later there were 150,000 cases. Some experts say that that illustrates the extent of the problem. Now the children can be treated with drugs and their condition improved.

Others say it proves nothing – except that children who do not behave as we think they should are now deemed to be 'suffering from a syndrome' and prescribed drugs to change their behaviour. Many of the greatest men in history showed all the symptoms of ADHD. We might wonder what would have become of them had they been treated with drugs to 'cure' their symptoms. Among them were Beethoven, Einstein, Frank Lloyd Wright, Picasso and Thomas Edison.

I don't know who is right. I do know that when the experts or the advertising men dig into their bag of words and create a new condition or a new syndrome we need to be on our guard. It is too easy to allow it to enter the bloodstream of our common language. Where once we might have used the language of 'being' or 'doing', we increasingly talk of 'getting' something. This has a big effect on how we behave. As soon as we can say he's 'got' it – whatever 'it' may be – discussion closes down.

No one is much interested in talking about chickenpox because we know what it is and what causes it. There is no more to say. But there is a vast amount to say about naughty children, for instance, and why they are naughty. By creating a new condition and applying it so widely, we bring the discussion to a close. In the United States five times as much Ritalin is prescribed as in the rest of the world combined. 'Yes, little Nigel suffers from ADHD, but he's on the latest drug now so everything's fine.' No, it's not. It's deeply worrying.

As for me, well, I'm a bit worried too. In the summer of 2004 a report was published of a study that looked at data on 200,000 men in seventeen countries and their various illnesses. It showed they were more likely to get ill than women. Dr Alan White of Leeds University, who led the study, said, 'We need to consider if men are more fragile than women or if being a man, in itself, is a disease.' But of course it is. Now, what's the cure?

See SEB!

So how are you feeling? Yes, you, dear reader. Just take a minute, as vicars sometimes say, to think about yourself. Pretty pleased with ourselves, are we? Well, in my case it depends. Some days I'll spend three hours in the *Today* studio and go home thinking I did a reasonably good job. Other days – too many of them – I leave wondering why I ever became a journalist in the first place. If I am incapable, after forty-five years in the business, of doing a half-way decent interview with a not-very-bright politician I really should pack it in and grow carrots.

This seems to me a fairly normal state. I am suspicious of people (and I doubt there are many of them) who never question their ability or even their qualifications for occupying their small space on this planet. It's called lack of self-esteem and anybody who does not experience it from time to time is either a smug, self-satisfied moron or on some pretty powerful drugs. But now 'lack of self-esteem' has become a syndrome.

'Self-esteem' is an expression we scarcely used a generation ago. As Frank Furedi points out, in the book whose prose I was so rude about earlier, the Factiva research organisation searched 300 British newspapers between 1980 and 2001 looking for the term. In 1980 there was not a single reference. In 1986 there were three and in 1990 it had risen to 103. In 2000 there were 3,328. But that's only the half of it.

We now have a self-esteem map – courtesy of the Demos think tank, which did the research. It shows the areas of the country where self-esteem is lowest and highest. It's lowest in the Midlands and highest in East Anglia, if you really want to know. The research was paid for by the Cosmetic Toiletry and Perfumery Association and its director general, Chris Flowers, says it provides 'hard evidence of how the nation views its self-esteem'. I promise you I am not making this up.

Demos recommends – and you will have no trouble believing this bit – that the government should help people build self-esteem. It suggests activities such as sport, art and music. But surely that doesn't go nearly far enough to address this crisis. What we really need is a Self-esteem Tsar with a team of civil servants (to be known as self-esteem boosters or SEBs for short) whom we can call whenever we're feeling a bit short of self-esteem. They could have their very own advertising slogan:

Feeling blue? SEB's for you!

It is possible, I suppose, that there has been a massive rise in the number of people who think they're pretty worthless. Maybe reality television has done it. Maybe we all watch those strange people on *Big Brother* and 'celebrity' shows and ask ourselves, 'Oh, God, why aren't I a celebrity too? I'm a failure!' But somehow I doubt it.

It is more likely that the word 'self-esteem' has become a part of our vocabulary and therefore part of our world. It is another 'condition' – only in this case it's something we *need* to have rather than something we didn't know we were suffering from. The effect is the same. We have been captured by the words and the words have persuaded us that there may be something wrong with us.

Stressed Out

All this is linked to the way 'stressed out' has replaced expressions that might have been used by an earlier generation: 'fed up' and its partner 'snap out of it'.

Clearly there are people who are clinically depressed and they need all the expert help they can get. It would be as silly to tell them to snap out of it as it would to tell a man with two broken legs to go for a brisk walk. But that is different from this:

> A quarter of children aged between four and six say they are 'stressed out', and the proportion rises to just over half of children under 16, reported a survey . . .

That appeared in the *Guardian* in March 2004. Put aside the horrible language (why stressed 'out' as opposed to simply stressed?) and think about the content. As I write this I am recovering from a birthday party: thirteen four-year-olds running riot in my garden. I try to imagine any one of them, let alone four of them, looking up, nodding sadly and saying yes, they are stressed out – just before they hurtle off again to see if they can bury the cat in the compost heap.

There will, no doubt, be tears before bedtime.

But 'stressed out' four-year-olds? They don't have even the vaguest concept of what it might mean unless they are told – and then told they 'have' it.

It is true that we put more pressure on small children in school than is probably good for them, but what is ludicrous is that we should bundle all the varied experiences of young life into a parcel called 'stress' and then imagine that they are carrying it. Remember, this article did not report what adults thought about the children: it purported to reveal what children thought about themselves. I do not believe the results of that survey. And if we did not have that new phrase in our vocabulary it could not have been used. But now it exists and otherwise perfectly sensible people like *Guardian* journalists report it in a way that encourages us to believe it.

It is the same process that turns tiredness into 'daily fatigue' – and it usually leads to the same solution: take a pill. It seems that all experience can be given a term and turned into a condition. I saw a book in a local bookshop the other day: *Love Sick: Love as a Mental Illness*. Even in the interests of research, I could not bear to pick it up. The next step, no doubt, will be a pill to cure love. Someone's going to make a lot of money out of this.

New words are essential to describe new things, new experiences. In Shakespeare's time there were something like forty thousand words in the vocabulary. He used about twenty thousand, which was a remarkable number for those days. Today we have about half a million words and we use twice as many as Shakespeare – though not always as creatively. There is a difference between inventing a new word to accommodate something that did not exist – 'computer' or 'television' – and inventing a new word to persuade us that something exists when it may well not. What it amounts to is manipulation – whether at the hands of the advertisers who create the phrase to sell an idea, a drugs manufacturer trying to sell its pills or a doctor desperate for something to tell a patient.

All this is having its effect on our national consciousness. A doctor who works in hospitals and prisons and writes under the pseudonym Theodore Dalrymple wrote about happiness. 'In the past fourteen years,' he said, 'I have heard only one patient say he was unhappy. He was a prisoner who wanted to go to another prison to be near his family. Otherwise all considered themselves to be depressed – suffering from a specific condition which it was the doctor's responsibility to relieve.' That, as Dr Dalrymple put it, relieves the patient of the painful duty of examining himself and trying to change.

Community Spirit

Community is a good thing, right? Most of us want to live in communities where people help each other out from time to time and where we can feel at home. We used to call it being good neighbours but, no matter, community is a perfectly good word – except that it is now used so widely and indiscriminately that we are manipulated into thinking communities exist where they do not.

We now have the 'gay community' – or so it is claimed. It is used all the time in the media. Friends of mine who are gay say it is a deeply suspect notion. Gay men may spend a lot of time with other gay men, and lesbians with other lesbians, but neither group mixes much as a group with the other. In that sense there certainly isn't a homosexual community.

Obviously some gay activists come together to form organisations, but they are a minority. Political activists always are. There is also a thriving club scene for young gay men in every big city, but that's hardly a community either: more an opportunity for commercial interests to cash in on the pink pound. And there are gay publications, mostly focused on what individual gays might want and need as consumers, rather than the concerns of any community. And . . . er . . . that's it. Or so I am told by gay friends. Yet the rest of us go on talking about the 'gay community' as though its existence were an established fact. It's not.

Communities that do not exist are springing up everywhere. People who rail against speed cameras or the price of petrol are often now referred to as the 'motoring community'. Presumably it is made up of those people who hate all the other motorists on the road because they are causing traffic jams or overtaking them – or just existing. Some community.

'Partnership' is another new one and it is usually just as daft. We are now invited to regard those who try to make us stick to the speed limit as 'speed-camera partnerships'. There are forty-two around the country, you'll be delighted to know. The notion behind this bizarre creation is that the police and local authority in any given area are working together. If we think of them as a partnership, it seems we will be less likely to regard them as the spawn of Satan. Hence this from *The Times*:

> Cameras had been placed where there was a part-nership concern about road safety.

A 'partnership concern'. What a wonderful piece of spin. Next time you get a ticket for doing 31 m.p.h. in a built-up area you will not conjure up images of some hatchet-faced sadist in a uniform plotting with lickspittle council officials how to rob you of another fifty quid and ban you from driving to visit your sick granny. Instead you will think of the gently smiling partners concerned only for your safety.

Their meeting probably began with a few softly spoken comments and maybe a little silent reflection on the victims of speed hogs and then – oh, so reluctantly – an agreement that, yes, perhaps it would be necessary to put another camera on that straight stretch of road where no one has ever been injured but people have been observed going a little faster than the legal limit. After all . . . one day . . . who knows? There might be an accident.

Well, maybe that's how it is, but I doubt it. On balance I'd prefer to believe in the tooth fairy. These new phrases are created not to accommodate the changing world but to change our attitudes. The word for it is 'manipulation'. Then again, perhaps I'm just a little peeved at being excluded from a reception in the House of Commons organised by the National Association of Local Councils. A friend showed me his invitation. The purpose of the event was to celebrate

Making Community Delivery Happen – Maximising First Tier Potential with the Community Delivery Agenda.

Hurrah!

Ludwig Wittgenstein said one of the things we had to be on the look-out for was the tendency of language to 'bewitch' thought. People who use language to manipulate us have learned that lesson well. Once they have conned us into believing that something exists which probably does not, they then have to con us into giving it our approval – or, sometimes, our disapproval. For this purpose they know there are really only two kinds of words: hurrah words and boo words. 'Community' and 'partnership' are obvious examples of hurrah words. The ultimate boo word is 'evil'.

This is an interesting word because it belongs to a world that, for many people, no longer exists. It presupposes that we believe in the Devil. Yet many people who do not believe in the Devil are ready to use the word when they could use something far less loaded: 'wicked'. The problem with 'wicked' is that it raises questions and invites discussion. Why did he do that wicked thing? Why is he like that? But 'evil' closes down discussion. He is evil because he is evil. He belongs, as it were, to the Devil's party. End of story. That's why 'evil' is such a useful boo word – even for those who don't have a belief in the Devil to justify it.

Too much of what passes for public debate

consists simply of firing off hurrah and boo words. Try this small group of hurrah words:

new
modern
efficient
scientific
progressive
economic
deserving

They tend to come in packages. If it is 'new', then it is also modern and efficient and naturally we approve. These are roughly equivalent boo words:

old
outdated
outmoded
traditional
emotional
wasteful
privileged

So we all know where we are, then? Well, not quite. Because there is another set of hurrah words that tend also to rally us. Words like:

authentic
natural
real
healthy
organic

And when you look at that list you see they are
pretty much the enemies of the original hurrah list
and live more comfortably with the first set of boo
words. Why should 'old' be a boo word? Who would
not want an 'old master' hanging in the living room?
Why is 'scientific' a hurrah word? To many people
it implies a mechanistic, insensitive approach to life.
'Emotion' may be good. We all get emotional over
a newborn baby. 'Progressive' is bad if progressive
laws mean the baby might have been aborted. It
depends, as they say, where you're coming from.

The manipulators know that if they find the right
hurrah words they are half-way to catching us. The
cleverest of them know that tapping into both sets
is even more effective. Try this sales pitch from an
outfit called Lakeland Willow Spring Water:

Containing the unique ingredient, trace salicin,
Willow is naturally occurring spring water that
originates from the Cartmel Valley in the Lake District. Enjoyed by thousands of people who believe
it holds the key to good health and well-being,

Willow is the proof that 'Mother Nature really does know best'.

Terrific. Let's hear it for good old Mother Nature. You can see Prince Charles ordering a case even as I write. We're talking 'natural' here and 'authentic' – two of the best hurrah words when you're peddling this sort of thing. But what's this? The water is also . . . 'the UK's only natural acquaceutical'. Now where did that word come from? I could find it only on American websites, so that might explain why I had never heard it before. Its purpose is transparent. It carries the echo of 'pharmaceutical' and, with it, the rubber-stamping of 'scientific' methods. This is clever stuff. It creates two images simultaneously: Mother Nature at her most benign, wandering the fresh green hills of the Lake District, and clever men in white coats ensuring everything is 'scientifically' sound.

Bastards!

That word probably caught your attention. It caught the nation's when John Major was prime minister and he used it in an unguarded moment, thinking the microphones had been switched off. He was referring to colleagues who'd been swearing their undying loyalty in public and stabbing him in the back in private – in other words, doing what politicians do. But when did you last hear it used in its dictionary sense, to describe children born out of wedlock? Can't remember, eh? Neither can I. We don't do it any longer. It would be deemed not politically correct.

I said earlier that 'evil' is the ultimate boo word. The ultimate boo phrase is 'politically correct' or, as the tabloids invariably have it, 'political correctness gone mad'. Use the phrase to attack what someone else has said and you're home and dry. That's usually the end of the argument. It should not be.

I once wrote an article for the *Sunday Times* about a child called Naomi. She was born with microcephalus, cerebral palsy and epilepsy. Neither her brain nor her body would ever develop in any normal way. She would always be doubly incontinent, unable to walk more than a few steps, unable to resist hurting herself and hurling herself out of her wheelchair. She would weep with the pain she inflicted on herself, but would be unable to stop. Her mental age would never advance beyond that of a baby. Unsurprisingly, Naomi's mother realised from the start that she could not cope with her.

But two wonderful people, Brian and Sandra Perkins, took an interest in her when she was six weeks old. They grew to love this wretched little scrap of humanity and eventually, in spite of many bureaucratic hurdles, managed to adopt her – even though they had two children of their own and no money to spare. Their lives were devoted to Naomi.

They are the sort of people who should be honoured by the state. Instead they were treated shabbily by an unfeeling bureaucracy over their entitlement to modest respite care. I wrote about Naomi and, as a result, generous readers donated many thousands of pounds to a children's hospice. The Perkinses would take no money for themselves, although they did accept a new wheelchair for Naomi. The cabinet minister responsible for the rules affecting people like the Perkinses promised they would be changed. It's not often that newspaper columns actually change anything, but then again it's not often columnists come across such appalling examples of the state failing such good people.

A few weeks later I was asked by Scope, the excellent charity that helps children like Naomi, to help them draw attention to their work and chair a discussion. Several people in the audience thanked me for the column – but I was also attacked for having described Naomi in the newspaper as 'dreadfully disabled'. Such language, it seems, will not do. Naomi is 'differently' abled, it seems. How did I know that this child saw herself in the same light as I was describing her? It's not often I am lost for words, but the only phrase that would come to my mind (happily I kept my mouth shut) was . . . yes . . . 'political correctness gone mad'. As I write I have a newspaper in front of me with an advertisement for Scope on its front page. It shows a young woman in a wheelchair and asks the reader to consider whether she is a

> victim of sexism . . . ageism . . . racism or [in highlighted type] . . . disablism.

Again that clichéd phrase pops into my head. But I wonder. Does anyone doubt that we treat disabled people with greater respect and afford them more dignity than we did a generation ago? I don't mean just the physical improvements – wheelchair ramps, reserved parking spaces – but the less tangible. The days of the patronising 'Does he take sugar?' approach are almost behind us. This would not have happened without a pretty fierce assault by people like Scope both on attitudes and language. It's not long ago that 'spastic' was used routinely to describe people with a specific disability. Then it was adopted as a form of abuse by morons and misguided children thinking it sounded cool. That will die out eventually too.

To the extent that political correctness exists, it relies heavily on people manipulating the language.

But at least it's out there in the open so that we can see what's going on and can have an argument about it if we disagree. In May 2004 the Judicial Studies Board published a hefty document called the *Equal Treatment Bench Book*. It was a guide to the language judges should use in court. They should not, for instance, say 'man and wife' because it implies a particular relationship between the couple. Well, yes, it would, wouldn't it? 'Common sense' was not deemed advisable. Quite so.

Almost every newspaper ridiculed the document and, inevitably, it was dismissed as yet another example of political correctness gone mad. That's a pity because it raised some serious issues. I'm baffled as to why 'wheelchair-bound' should be deemed unacceptable and 'wheelchair user' acceptable, but there is a very good case for not referring to 'the disabled'. People with some form of disability are not automatically members of a subgroup of society, which is what 'the disabled' implies. We don't talk about 'the red-headed' or 'the left-handers'. Why should someone who has to use a wheelchair become 'the disabled'? And why should anyone be described as a 'second-generation immigrant'? It is not 'politically correct' to object to this sort of thing. It is, to speak the unspeakable, common sense.

Gay Times

Professor Deborah Cameron of Oxford University makes a convincing case in her book *Verbal Hygiene* that the notion of political correctness is largely an invention of its enemies. It is a familiar political ploy. First, take control of defining your political enemy's identity, then attack it to your heart's content. This is what has happened to many people who have honestly and openly tried to influence the way we use language.

Shifts in society's values are always controversial. Not everyone agrees with the changes and even those who do tend to move at different speeds. Often the rows focus on the change in language as a surrogate for argument about the real issue. The classic case of that was the row over the word 'gay'.

There will always, I suppose, be people who regard homosexuality as a condition of moral degeneracy rather than the way others just happen to be. When homosexuals began seriously campaigning against it, language was one of their prime weapons. They wanted to get rid of 'queer' and 'poof', with their overtones of moral disapproval, and substitute a neutral word. They chose 'gay' and they used it relentlessly until it became the standard.

There were plenty of people – and not only those

who wanted to keep the moral stigma alive – who objected that a perfectly good word was being hijacked. How very sad that we can no longer have a gay old time, they said. Of course, we've got nothing against homosexuals, but really it's not right that they should steal this delightful word.

Well, so be it. We can object to the way certain words are used until our dying day, but usage will determine the outcome. If we can't persuade enough people to agree with us, we lose. This was one the gays won.

Interestingly those ugly old words – 'queer' and 'poof' – have undergone a change too. 'Queer' is still used (almost always under the breath) by those who insist that gay people are moral degenerates, but it is kept alive by militant homosexuals too. They think the assimilation of gay people into main-stream society has gone too far. They want to retain a distinctive identity, not based on a moral differ-ence but on differences of lifestyle. They want to keep 'queer' as its badge.

At the other end of the spectrum 'poof' has been revived as the cosy word to reflect total assimilation. The backing group for Jonathan Ross's television chat show call themselves Four Poofs and a Piano. But I hear that when they tried to register themselves as a company with this name, the authorities were uneasy. They were told it was discriminatory and homophobic – proving that *is* possible to be more Catholic than the Pope.

He or She ... or What?

The other great social and linguistic campaign of recent years has been fought by feminists. As with most campaigns based on fairness, it moved quickly from a relatively small group of activists to embrace women everywhere. They objected – among many other things – to the automatic assumption of male dominance and superiority that riddles the language. Why should you be referred to generically as 'he' if you are a woman? The problem comes when we look for an alternative. The radical feminist solution is to say that two can play at this game, so you would have something like:

A soldier's life can be tough. So she has to be physically fit.

What's wrong with that? Many women serve in the army. But it jars (as it is intended to) and it won't work in the long run because men serve in the army too.

There are ways round it:

A soldier's life is tough. So physical fitness is essential.

It works, but it's less direct and that sort of rearrangement is not always possible. An alternative is he/she, which is clumsy and downright ugly. S/he is even worse. That leaves one option and you hear it whenever you dial 1471 on the phone:

You were called at 5.32 p.m. today. The caller withheld their number.

Aargh! You don't have to be a strict grammarian to scream at the notion of using a plural pronoun to refer to a singular subject. But if you can think of another version you're a better man/woman than me. Sorry: woman/man. I suppose 'they' will be accepted into general usage as a singular pronoun alongside its use as the plural and people will stop complaining about it.

It has happened to 'chair', which is more or less accepted as the neutral version of chairman/woman, though some old fogies (and, yes, I am referring to me) still go to great lengths to avoid using it. Neither do I like 'spokesperson'. I can see no reason not to say spokesman or spokeswoman. Yet again, usage will win in the end.

The respect and status accorded to women matters a great deal; the merit of 'chair' versus 'chair-person' is a small matter. What should really exercise us is the attempt to use language to get us to adopt a particular approach without any argument over the substance of the case.

A friend has spent years teaching English to people for whom it is not their first language. When she did it abroad it was called Teaching English as a Foreign Language. Now she does it in London for immigrants and it is Teaching English as an Alternative Language. This annoys her and she has a point.

Immigration is a highly sensitive political issue. The government has decreed that people who want to come to live in this country must have, among other things, a basic grasp of English. Some people regard that as a form of discrimination. Whatever your view, there is an argument to be had. To suggest that learning English for these people is an option, when in fact it is a requirement, is at worst dishonest and, at best, a form of subterfuge. This is political correctness with a hidden motive and there is a lot of it about.

Some of it is just plain silly. The English National Opera banned new staff from using the word 'darling' with each other. It was deemed to constitute a form of sexual harassment. In the United States a white man who ran a municipal agency was forced to resign after he had described his budget as 'niggardly'. This is not only etymologically absurd, it is pernicious.

It would be futile and wrong to argue against the manipulation of language. All language manipulates in one sense or another. Listen to a child persuading his mother to let him stay up late or the salesman in a car showroom. What matters when we are discussing the big issues is that it should be above board. The manipulation to guard against is that which happens below the radar. Politicians know a thing or two about it.

CHAPTER FOURTEEN

The Twisted Words of Politics

It is taken as read that politicians use manipulative language. What else is 'spin' but manipulation? The word itself is relatively new to this country, though not the practice. Some of our best politicians have been famously plain speakers. Ask most people who was the greatest British foreign secretary of the twentieth century and the answer will almost certainly be Ernest Bevin, the self-taught former dockers' leader.

On one occasion, sailing across the Atlantic on one of the great liners, he was asked by the head waiter what he would care to have for dinner. 'Steak and newts!' came the peremptory reply. Utterly bewildered, the waiter retreated to the kitchen to find out if anyone could make head or tail of it. But no one could, so a more senior flunkey was dispatched to ask again. 'Steak and newts!' came the answer. It was only when the great man was prevailed on to point out on the menu what had taken his fancy that it was discovered he required a fillet steak and a bottle of Nuits-St-Georges.

He was much clearer in his political talk. Here he is, speaking in the House of Commons not long after first becoming foreign secretary in 1945:

> 'There never has been a war yet which, if the facts had been put calmly before the ordinary folk, could not have been prevented ... The common man, I think, is the greatest protection against war.'

This, of course, was in the days before dossiers. Later he summed up his approach in very simple terms indeed:

> 'My [foreign] policy is to be able to take a ticket at Victoria Station and go anywhere I damn well please.'

His plain-speaking did not mean he lacked political cunning. In good Labour Party style he harboured deep resentments against some of his fellow comrades, especially Herbert Morrison, Peter Mandelson's grandfather. When he was told that Morrison had described himself as his own worst enemy, Bevin muttered, 'Not while I'm alive he ain't!'

Yes, Minister

Lord knows what Bevin must have made of the language he encountered when first he strode into the Foreign Office. Diplomats are not well known for straight talking. It is not exactly that they lie – in spite of the observation four centuries ago that an ambassador is an honest man sent to lie abroad for the good of his country. In truth, they don't need to lie. Their training equips them to be economical with the truth in a way that makes it unnecessary.

Where parliamentarians enjoy obfuscation, diplomats revel in euphemism. The essential trick of this particular trade is never, ever, to say anything that might upset the horses. The ultimate compliment is to call someone a safe pair of hands. Ask these people the time of day and you are likely to be asked in return what time you would *like* it to be. They regard journalists, whose currency is controversy, as pond life. They deal with us only because they must. Running the press office at the Foreign and Commonwealth Office is usually regarded as a thoroughly disagreeable chore, to be completed with the minimum of embarrassment for as brief a period as possible before moving on to an ambassadorship, preferably somewhere civilised like Paris or Rome or Washington.

Journalists being briefed by a diplomat often feel

they inhabit a parallel universe – especially when it is about talks that have just taken place between our man and a foreign leader. If the two got on so well that they agreed on every single issue and ended up sending the civil servants out of the room while they enjoyed a passionate embrace on the office sofa, the discussions will be characterised (a favourite word in diplomat-speak) as 'constructive' and possibly 'fruitful'. If they agreed on absolutely nothing, clearly detested each other and spent the entire meeting swapping insults, the exchange will be described as 'useful'. If the foreign leader ends the meeting declaring war on Britain, journalists will be told the talks were 'frank'. The strongest word in the briefer's lexicon is 'unfortunate'. Obviously, that is reserved for dealings with the French.

In the parallel universe inhabited by diplomats – or diplomatists, as the stuffier of them would have it – time stands still. For once, it is not a cliché. If agreement cannot be reached by the deadline set for the talks, they will literally stop the clocks. It is unnerving to look at the clock on the wall of the conference room and see that the hands have not moved for the past eight hours.

Clever Lawyers

Politicians, of course, can be just as tricksy with words as diplomats, particularly if they are clever and are lawyers. Bill Clinton was both.

'I did not have sex with that woman'

is either a downright lie, or a brilliantly creative definition of 'sex', depending on your point of view. At one point in his travails over Monica Lewinsky, he actually told a grand jury: 'It depends what the meaning of "is" is . . .'

We have clever politicians of our own. The Tory MP David Willetts is known as 'Two Brains'. When he was a whip in John Major's government he got himself into a spot of bother over a note he had written. In it he had said that Sir Geoffrey Johnson-Smith, the Tory chairman of the House of Commons Committee on Members' Interests, 'wants our advice' over the Neil Hamilton cash-for-questions affair. This was thought most improper because the committee was supposed to be at arm's length from the government.

The note was leaked, of course, to the newspapers and Mr Willetts sought to get out of it in a most imaginative way. He tried to persuade us that when he had used the word 'want' he hadn't meant it in the modern, vulgar sense of 'need' (good gracious, no), but rather in the archaic and literary sense – the way you'd find it in Jane Austen – meaning 'lack'. Just as Mr Wickham in *Pride and Prejudice* 'wants' (lacks) breeding, so Sir Geoffrey 'wants' our advice, which was, of course, just how things should be.

I don't know what Ernie Bevin would have made of it but it did not save Mr Willetts's bacon.

Citizen Who?

But politics has changed enormously since Bevin was foreign secretary and Attlee was prime minister. The biggest change is the advent of television. Attlee once returned from a foreign trip and was approached by a young television reporter with a microphone. 'Sir, have you anything to say to the nation?' he asked. 'No,' said the great man, and walked away. Attlee's successors are about as likely to do that today as they are to snatch the microphone from the reporter and sing three verses of 'My Way'. Attlee could afford to ignore television. Modern politicians must bend to the demands of twenty-four-hour news.

Parliament has a vastly bigger audience now that its debates are televised than it ever had in the past and yet, curiously, it commands less attention than it ever has. Political campaigners have more or less given up knocking on doors and almost no one nips down to the town hall to hear their MP holding forth because that's been killed off too.

This means that politicians have both won and lost an audience. The audience they have won sits in front of a television and catches glimpses of them being interviewed. Sometimes it will endure a longish setpiece interview but there are precious few of them. That is the combined effect of the television controllers, who are terrified we will switch off if we are not instantly grabbed, and the politicians, who are terrified of saying anything interesting. The result is that the people who constitute the new audience have been converted from citizens into consumers. It's happening, one way and another, in many areas of our lives.

I once interviewed the man who runs the Inland Revenue. He referred to taxpayers as customers. Excellent, I said, in that case I shall take my business elsewhere. Will that be okay? He said no, it would not. In what sense, then, are we customers? What service are we buying and how do we exercise the choice implicit in being a customer? He thought I was being silly.

Poor people who need the help of Social Services are described as clients. Yet when they turn up at the offices to ask for help to buy a bed or a refrigerator, they are often faced with a civil servant sitting behind a reinforced-glass screen and must speak into a microphone. Not quite the same treatment that an advertising agency accords its clients, I think. The word is an abuse. There was even an attempt in the NHS to turn patients into clients, though that has been laughed out – so far. Watch for it slipping back again. And watch, too, for voters becoming clients. The politicians may not use the word yet, but it can't be far off: we are already 'consumers'. If you were listening to the *World at One* in May 2004 you would have heard this:

'We are looking at the market overall and looking to see what kite-marking arrangements can be made to help the public across the board ... The guiding principle throughout has been what helps the consumer in the market.'

Was this the editor of *Which?* telling us how the market in electric toasters should be regulated to protect us from dangerous wiring? It was not. It was the Rt Hon. the Lord Falconer, Lord Chancellor, Secretary of State for Constitutional Affairs, and close friend of the Prime Minister. What he was talking about was not toasters but his decision to retain and reform the system by which barristers become QCs.

It is true that in one sense we are customers of

QCs and, as consumers of legal services, we need protection. But the law is more than something we consume. It is about justice. It is our protection. It concerns a world in which we should go on thinking of ourselves as citizens rather than just customers. All of that applies equally to the world of politics.

Citizens Argue, Consumers Shop

The difference in name implies a wholly different activity. What you do with citizens is engage them in a debate. What you do with customers is flog them something. Selling is not the same thing as debating and debating is central to what the democratic system is supposed to be about. It means engaging with the other side. It is a dynamic activity. Positions have to be abandoned or advanced as they are tested in the exchange. Debate causes our understanding to move on. We all benefit by learning more as a result of the tussle between the debaters.

When Abraham Lincoln and his political adversary Stephen Douglas toured the state of Illinois in the senatorial election of 1858, debating with each other in public meetings, they formed a sort of double act. But the act was not the same performance repeated night after night. Each man had to modify his position in the light of the damage done to it in the previous day's encounter. That's why the

Lincoln–Douglas debates are still worth reading. They show how two immensely able politicians had to revise and develop their views as a result of having them tested in debate.

Selling doesn't work like that. Rival biscuit manufacturers don't debate with each other. They keep a close eye on what the competition is up to, but their engagement with their rivals is not public. It is done behind closed doors: the market research is pored over; focus group findings analysed; strategies developed to outwit the competitors. Modern politics is much closer to this model than to the public sparring of Lincoln and Douglas.

The Big Sell

Norman Fairclough, the professor of language in social life at Lancaster University, wrote a book a few years ago called *New Labour, New Language?* in which he said:

> The Government tends to act like a corporation treating the public as its consumers rather than its citizens.

But this tendency is not confined to one party. Charles Kennedy, the leader of the Liberal Democrats, accused Tony Blair of 'failing to sell a positive image' of Europe. The language of selling has been adopted by all politicians.

The effect on political language of our becoming customers goes further. Orwell's advice to 'let the meaning choose the word' falls on deaf ears in this climate. As the Australian journalist Don Watson puts it:

> In modern media-driven politics, words are chosen less for their meaning than for their ability to do the job.

And what is that 'job'? It is not to conduct an argument but to sell a message. Messages rather than arguments are what modern politics trades in. Alastair Campbell provided what were called 'message scripts' to direct the government's media operation of the day. Even as urbane and traditional a politican as the Liberal Democrats' foreign-affairs spokesman, Sir Menzies Campbell, a man rooted in the politics of debate, uses the language: '. . . we will continue to make sure those messages are properly promoted'.

Promotions are exactly what marketing departments employ to attract the attention of consumers. The language of commerce is the language of politics. And because that is how it now is, that is how it is reported. Here's Andrew Marr, the BBC's

political editor, reporting what was going on in
No. 10:

> 'They're selling different messages. They're selling
> the message "There's an exit strategy – we're on the
> way out" (Message One). And they're selling the
> message "We're not going to cut and run. We're
> sticking with the Iraqis; we're going to see this job
> through" as Tony Blair was saying (Message Two).'

It's the Message, Stupid

And what is the message? Well, mostly it is what
they think we want to hear. They find that out by
asking focus groups. The use of focus groups has
often been attacked in the belief that they are a
substitute for real political debate and proper
policy-making, but that's not strictly true. It is not
so much that they determine policy, although they
will clearly have an effect on it. What they do is tell
the politicians what language will sell the policies
and what won't.

The effect is that language has a different function in the new politics from the one it had in the
old. Then, it was tested in debate by the politicians.
Now it is tested in small groups of 'consumers'
by marketing people. Last week: Coca-Cola. This
week: hospital waiting lists.

Occasionally politicians and their acolytes will admit that there is a problem here. In May 2004 Geoff Mulgan, the former head of the policy unit in Downing Street, gave a lecture partly devoted to attacking the media for having abandoned the ethic of searching for the truth. He said:

'This ethical deficit at the core of the information society may be compounded by the increased volume of commercial communication, which, *like political communication* [my italics], indirectly promotes the idea that there are no truths, only strategies and claims.'

Commercial communication, of course, rests on slogans, not the truth. You cannot prove the truth of a claim that 'Coke Adds Life' or 'Persil Washes Whiter', nor can it be debated intelligently. You simply have to believe it or reject it. The same applies to the sort of political slogans that now pass for intelligent debate: 'for the many not the few'; 'in Europe but not run by Europe'; 'tough on crime and tough on the causes of crime'. Back in the mists of time when they were first coined, they may have had an accessible meaning and sparked our interest, but they have become political clichés. They are used simply to convey an impression.

It is the same with buzz words such as 'passion',

'commitment' and 'exciting', which are often used in spite of their real meaning rather than because of it. Do we really believe that the minister is passionate about his new policy and finds it exciting? Or do we believe that it may well have been devised to get the government out of a hole and will be jettisoned if things turn out differently from the way they fear?

The simplest words are often dumped. We all know what 'poor' means, but it is seldom used – especially when politicians are afraid to draw attention to, say, a widening gap between rich and poor. When they talk about dirt-poor countries such as Chad or Tanzania, they will use the word 'developing'. The implication is that they are gradually becoming richer. The truth is that most African countries are becoming even poorer. I'm sorry that the BBC has fallen for this and we have a 'developing-world correspondent'.

'Priority' is another popular word with politicians. They want us to think they give priority to whatever we might think is important. The problem is that we think lots of things are important. To give something priority means choosing between things – but in their world everything can be a priority. That's because they don't want to tell us they have chosen one thing over another. But if everything is a priority, nothing is.

Who's the Victim?

If political communication is effectively reduced to marketing messages, it's not surprising that politicians resort to the basic trick of manipulative language. I've already talked about the use of hurrah and boo words. Boo words are usually pretty transparent when politicians use them. Hurrah words can be more difficult to spot.

When a politician talks about 'modernising' the NHS the assumption is that we will approve. How can anyone be against modernising? You would not dream of buying a car with no heater or radio and brakes that make stopping on a wet road a triumph of hope over experience. Car design has been modernised and that is a good thing. So is central heating. And how about getting root-canal work done by a dentist who uses a drill operated by a foot pedal and hasn't heard of Novocaine?

Yet there are many aspects of the old-fashioned NHS of which you might have approved: ward sisters and matrons, maybe, for whom godliness came a poor second to cleanliness. But if you express any doubts you are dismissed as being 'against modernisation', which is, of course, a bad thing.

Some hurrah words are more insidious and difficult to spot. Take 'balance'. Politicians from all parties tell us endlessly that the criminal justice system needs 'rebalancing' in favour of the victim. That's a pretty safe position to defend. Surely we must all be on the side of victims. So if the system needs rebalancing in their favour let's get on with it.

But this is a manipulation of the word's meaning. Those famous scales in the hands of Blind Justice are not meant to symbolise balancing the interests of the victim against the interests of the accused. They are there to weigh the evidence of the prosecution against that of the defence. That's it. The interests of the victim are no different from the interests of society as a whole: to see justice done, nothing more and nothing less. Victims might well want revenge – it is the most human of instincts – but the judicial system should not. One of its purposes is to prevent it.

What is generally meant by 'rebalancing' the system is making it easier to get a conviction by lowering the burden of proof – by tipping the scales a bit. It means that fewer of the guilty will be acquitted. It also means that more of the innocent will be convicted. There may or may not be a good case for doing this but it has nothing to do with redressing the balance in favour of a victim. How would sending an innocent man to jail do that? But, of course, no politician would couch the argument in those terms and expect to get away with it – so the call is for 'rebalancing' instead.

Possibly the most famous hurrah phrase for a generation was Tony Blair's 'tough on crime: tough on the causes of crime'. How can anyone argue with such a sentiment? But every police officer, judge, magistrate, probation officer and mugger's victim will tell you that the way to be tough on crime is to catch the criminals. The problem with 'catch more crooks' as a soundbite is that it promises a specific action and politicians can be held to account if a promise is not kept. Hurrah words are safer. The trick is to use a word that sounds dynamic to convey the impression of real dynamism.

Whose Choice?

In 2004 politicians discovered a new hurrah word: choice. Again, how can anyone be against choice? Quite easily, is the answer. It's good to be able to choose between cornflakes and porridge for breakfast but it's ghastly to stand in a supermarket (especially with a demanding child) and be faced with a hundred different kinds of breakfast cereal. One of the best journalists I have ever worked with wore the same clothes every day: grey trousers, pale blue shirt and, in the winter, dark blue sweater. He had no interest in clothes and could see no point in wasting time every morning deciding what to wear. He had more important things to think about.

But politicians persuaded themselves – and tried to persuade us – that we all want choice and choice became the new hurrah word. Things got a bit sticky when the implications began to sink in. Choice is important only if we are able to choose something – school, hospital, GP – that is better than what we have already. So what do we do with the rejected school or hospital? Close it down? Or will this new competition raise standards everywhere? The problem with this argument is that people tend to be a little uneasy with the word 'competition'. It means someone must lose and it has become a bit of a boo word. So choice it is.

Only in Moderation

Politicians (and journalists) love to divide the world into extremists and moderates. One of the two precepts the ancient Greeks laid down for a good life was 'nothing in excess', so pinning the label 'extremist' on someone tells us all we need to know about them. It is a boo word. 'Mainstream' politicians are, of course, moderate. Otherwise they wouldn't be mainstream, would they? It is a hurrah word.

That leaves the radicals with nowhere to go. So they get called extremists and we don't need to bother paying attention to what they say. It makes life so much easier for the mainstream moderates.

This is a game virtually all politicians try to play. Labour wants us to think the Tories are extremist in their public-spending policies. The Tories want us to think UKIP is extremist on Europe. The Lib-Dems want us to think Tony Blair is extremist on Iraq. Meanwhile they themselves are all moderate, naturally.

The trouble is that extremists can often be right and moderates wrong. We think of Neville Chamberlain these days as an appeaser and, therefore, a baddy. But in the 1930s he was a moderate and, therefore, a goody. It was not that he denied the Nazi threat: it was simply that he favoured a 'moderate' way of dealing with it. Churchill, by contrast, was an extremist (a baddy) and, for a long time, ostracised by the moderates. Yet he happened to be right.

These labels are intended to manipulate us. The politicians who use them are saying – sometimes specifically, usually by implication – that there is no need to look behind them to see what is being offered. Why bother? They're extreme views. If we could get away from these manipulative labels we might be able to hear what everyone is actually saying.

I Can't Say It Too Often

The modern political message must be short and sharp and simple. That way it can be drilled into us. So if virtue in the old politics of debate lay in cogency of argument, in the new politics it lies in repetition. Say it often enough and we will get the message. That is the first law not just of marketing but of propaganda. As Goebbels said: 'A lie that is repeated a thousand times becomes the truth.'

Goebbels and his propaganda machine lied. Most politicians in democratic societies do not – or, at least, they try hard not to. With some it is because they think it is wrong to lie; with others it is because they are smart enough to know they might be caught out. In other words, they're pretty much like everyone else. But, boy, have they learned the value of repetition. The master in modern politics is Gordon Brown.

Several years ago I had a chat with him after a particularly gruelling interview, in which I had got absolutely nowhere, and pointed out that he had an irritating habit. At some point in the interview he would invariably seize on a question and say, 'I've got three points to make on that.' And off he would go, making the points about something or other (usually prudence in those days) that he had made a thousand times before while you sat there waiting for his little lecture to come to an end.

He seemed a bit surprised when I objected to it and I got the impression he would mend his ways. He did. The next time I interviewed him I asked whatever the trigger question was and the answer came back, 'I've got five points to make . . .' I wouldn't swear to this, but I think there was a grin in his voice.

All the evidence suggests that Mr Brown simply doesn't care whether he bores us with his use of language. On one level there's no reason why he should. Kenneth Clarke, Brown's predecessor, couldn't help but entertain. He was the light to Brown's shade. With him, the interviewer was never quite sure which way it would go. With Brown there is only ever one way: his way. He knows what he wants to say and he says it. If that means repeating the same mantras – 'an end to boom and bust'; 'put the public finances on a sound footing'; 'locking in stability' – then so be it. All he wants to do is get his message across.

At the time of writing he is still the Chancellor. It will be interesting to see if he uses the same technique if he finds himself occupying the house next door.

Beating About with Bush

George W. Bush is a master of the language. Yes, that is what I wrote and there's no need to read the sentence again. I mean, of course, the language of political manipulation. We can all have hours of fun ridiculing the way he massacres English but, to use one of his own expressions, it is a great mistake to misunderestimate him merely because he is in-articulate.

Take the way he uses words such as 'democracy' and 'freedom'. You don't need to be a student of political philosophy to know what a multitude of meanings and nuance those words have gathered over the last 2500 years. Democracy has more forms than the tax office; freedom is as complex a notion as truth. But all that nuance is swept aside by Mr Bush. He fires off the words as though they were dum-dum bullets that splatter on impact and carry only one meaning – one that is utterly unambiguous. Repetition has taken them beyond cliché. They have become zombified words whose meaning is no longer the point. They are mantras to be chanted. That is now their job.

This is deliberate. It means that it is effectively impossible to question what they mean. Why would anyone want to? 'Freedom and democracy' are what Americans believe in and there is no longer any need to think about it. Anyone who raises his hand, however tentatively, and asks, 'Excuse me, but . . .' must be an enemy of freedom and of democracy. Why would anyone question the meaning of the words, except to undermine them?

This incantation of freedom and democracy serves the now familiar trick of dividing people into two camps. There are those who defend the great, all-American values and there are those who want to carry on the argument about what they mean. In other words, there are good, decent patriots and there are the enemies of freedom and democracy. They are, to coin a phrase, for us or against us.

In Bush's vocabulary democracy and freedom are the ultimate hurrah words. They are used in direct contradiction to the ultimate boo word: evil. Those who question freedom and democracy automatically find themselves on the axis of evil.

The Unelected Democrat

When words are manipulated to this extent they can be used regardless of their real meaning. Thus Hamid Karzai was called the 'democratic' President of Afghanistan long before there was any election in the country. Now, Mr Karzai may be a very fine fellow indeed, but the one thing he was not, at the time the description was conferred on him, was a democratically elected leader. He was, though, a friend of America and an enemy of the evil Taliban and that was enough to qualify him as a democrat.

As for the terrorists who attacked the Twin Towers, this is what Bush said of them:

'They hate us because we are free.'

It is hard to know what this means. Bush might mean the terrorists hate Americans because they envy them the freedom that they do not have. That seems unlikely. There are dozens of targets they might have chosen on 11 September. America is not the only 'free' country in the world. But I am taking the words literally. I am falling into the trap of supposing the job they are doing bears any relationship to their literal meaning. Instead, words are being moved around irrespective of their meaning to create an effect. The equation is a simple and effective one: 'They hate us (true) + We are free (hurrah word) = applause.'

Triangulating Language

Language is used by some politicians to create a Manichean world divided into two camps. But there is a different kind of manipulation that seeks to achieve the opposite effect. Its purpose is to conjure

up a world in which there appears to be no oppo-
sition at all. Faced with two distinct philosophies,
it works out a third position and claims to offer all
the benefits of both. It is called – a wonderful
addition to the political vocabulary of the recent
past – 'triangulation'. The absolutist language of
George Bush turns words like 'freedom' and 'evil'
into rocks too hard to crack, too opaque to exam-
ine. The language of triangulation denies the reality
of the distinction between words and turns them
into sand that slips through the fingers. One makes
words mean nothing. The other makes them mean
anything.

The ultimate effect is the same: words cannot be
used as they should be. They should convey clear,
distinct meaning and they should be the tools of
argument. Instead they turn into brochures in a
salesman's briefcase – to be dished out to the
unwary householder who happens to open the door
when the bell rings. Instead of an argument, you
may end up with double-glazing you didn't even
know you wanted.

My Way?

In Britain triangulation was the basis of the Third
Way, and the Third Way was the ideology of New
Labour. So there you have three new political

phrases in one short sentence. New Labour: New Language. The wonder of it all is that no one has ever seemed absolutely certain what the Third Way is. If anyone can be said to be its intellectual god-father it is Anthony Giddens, the former director of the London School of Economics. Here is how he described it almost ten years after it first struggled into this rough old world:

> The Third Way, as I have always understood it, is simply a label for the renewal of social democracy.

It's the 'as I have always understood it' that is so endearing. This is a clever and an honest man speaking. You want to say, 'My dear chap, if *you* are not quite sure what it is, then what hope is there for the rest of us?' In his book *New Labour, New Language?* Professor Norman Fairclough describes the effect of the philosophy on the language of the party:

> The phrase 'not only ... but also' pervades the political discourse of New Labour in a variety of expressions ... which both draws attention to assumed incompatibilities, and denies them.

Here's an example of it from the Mandelson/ Liddle book I quoted earlier:

New Labour believes that it is possible to combine a free market economy with social justice; liberty of the individual with wider opportunities for all; One Nation security with efficiency and competitiveness; rights with responsibilities; personal self-fulfilment with strengthening the family; effective government and decisive political leadership with a new constitutional settlement and a new relationship of trust between politicians and the people; a love of Britain with a recognition that Britain's future has to lie in Europe.

In its own way this closes down argument as effectively as President Bush spouting mantras about freedom and democracy. If all those things can be combined, there is no need for any argument. Let's just have the lot. The same tentative voice that says, 'Excuse me, but how . . . ?' is likely to be dismissed again – not, this time, as an enemy of freedom, but as an enemy of optimism and of hope.

These two strategies set up two distinct vocabularies of manipulation for avoiding argument and deploying language for the purposes of political salesmanship. The first divides the world into camps. It sees the problems we face as the result of the hostile actions of shadowy enemies (evil-doers, enemies of freedom) and speaks a language of confrontation, of toughness, of crackdowns and the like. The second regards the world as essentially a harmonious place, sees our problems as caused by impersonal forces (change, globalisation) and speaks the language of community and partnership. Both are highly partial and tendentious and neither gives an account of how complex the world really is.

But what is really interesting is that politicians move between these two vocabularies at will, depending on what suits their interests at the time. George Bush is associated very much with the first vocabulary, but when he was running for office in 2000 he was speaking the second. He was the champion of 'compassionate conservatism' who wanted America to have a foreign policy that was 'strong but humble'.

Then he discovered how ruthless terrorists could be and how vulnerable was the United States. But the world had not changed. The terrorists had always been out there. They'd tried to blow up the Twin Towers years earlier. They had just got much better at committing mass murder. It goes to show that we should always be wary of allowing a politician's language to define for us how we should imagine the world may actually be.

Phoney War

Politicians love using 'war' as a metaphor. It conveys the impression that they are tough, no-nonsense leaders who are decisive and determined to defeat the problems that confront us. So there is not only a war on drugs, there is the war on crime, the war on want – even a war on obesity. But the metaphor bewitches thought.

Drugs provide a good example of that. It is a commonplace of political life that we are engaged in a 'war on drugs'. The language used is almost always that of confrontation. The drug barons and criminal cartels need to be 'taken on'; there must be 'crackdowns'. The danger with that sort of language is that it can close off debate. It is virtually impossible to have any serious discussion in Britain on the merits or otherwise of legalising drugs. To talk of legalising drugs is to admit defeat because we are engaged in a 'war'. We cannot 'surrender'. We must not be 'defeated'.

This loose use of the war metaphor can lead to collateral damage. When he occupied the White House, Ronald Reagan was mostly kept out of reach of the press except on carefully managed setpiece occasions. Once in a while reporters managed to get near enough to shout a question – usually when Reagan's helicopter blades were whirring. He would cup his hand round his ear and offer a rueful grin as if to say, 'Darn it! Can't quite make out what you're saying.' But sometimes it worked, usually as he was getting into his limo: 'Mr President, sir,' shouted one reporter over the heads of the secret service. 'What's happened to the war on poverty?'

'Gee,' said a typically genial, bemused-looking Reagan, pausing for thought. 'I guess poverty won.'

Which brings us to a different kind of war: the 'War on Terror'.

A War by Any Other Name

The defining event of the last half-century was the Cold War. The defining event of the new century is the 'War on Terror'. Both phrases are examples of the manipulative power of language. The Cold War was not a war but a policy of containment designed to prevent war. To the extent that it ever became a real war, it was fought by proxy states of the great powers in some of the most benighted corners of the world – mostly in Africa. In the end the Soviet empire was not defeated by the West but by itself. But the notion of the West 'at war' was politically valuable. People who think their very survival is at stake do not balk at military expansion and the vast amounts of money needed. In time of war we think differently.

So it is with the War on Terror. The point has been made many times that you cannot wage war on an abstract noun, yet the metaphor is a powerful one – far more useful than, say, a 'War on Terrorists', which would require specific victories such as the capture of Osama Bin Laden to justify its existence. A former chairman of the Joint Intelligence Committee, Dame Pauline Neville-Jones, warned about the dangers implicit in the language. She said its use 'confused the information element', as did expressions such as 'hearts and minds' and 'battle of ideas'.

There is another danger in this language. Repeat it often enough and people forget it is a metaphor and take it literally. It creates a number of assumptions. One is that 'terror' can somehow be defeated. Another is that military action is the only way of bringing about that defeat.

Both those assumptions are nonsense. Terrorism has been with us, in one form or another, since we crawled out of the primordial sludge and will be with us still when we creep back into it. That is, of course, unless we manage to create a society so perfect that no single group will ever bear such a grudge against another group that it is prepared to use force against it.

As with the Cold War, the War on Terror is a useful metaphor for politicians. We now know that

American neo-conservatives had decided long before 11 September that Saddam Hussein should be dealt with. It makes it much easier to persuade people to support military action if they are already using the language of war.

'Rogue states' is useful in the same way. Once the phrase becomes part of our vocabulary and loses its inverted commas we no longer have to worry about what it means. We know all we need to know. The rogue states are beyond the pale. They are outlaws. Implicit is the notion that they cannot be dealt with through the usual means of dialogue and negotiation. Very often we add to the picture by describing their leaders as mad and beyond the reach of rational self-interest. Obviously the only thing they understand is force or the threat of it. There are two problems with this sort of language. One is that it is rarely true: despotic leaders of 'rogue states' have a habit of behaving extremely rationally (if savagely) when their own interests are threatened. The other is that the language suddenly becomes out of place when our own interests change.

Language Labels

Libya was dubbed a rogue state and Colonel Gaddafi a mad dictator, yet Tony Blair found himself taking tea with Gaddafi in his tent in the Libyan desert. Language that labels and does not define is a dangerous tool. Saddam Hussein deserved all the terrible things that were said about him, but we used different language when he was our ally and we sold him arms. Iran was placed by George Bush on the 'axis of evil', but the British Foreign Office preferred to treat its leaders with respect.

The government of Sudan was said to be responsible for what was described by international agencies as the worst humanitarian crisis in the world in 2004. A million people were driven from their homes in Darfur, tens of thousands butchered, countless women raped. When a British government minister was asked about it he said the Sudanese government was 'in denial'. It was an interesting use of a phrase more often heard on the psychiatrist's couch.

If we are at war and our survival is threatened by an identifiable enemy, the propagandists have a clear job to do. When the language of war is used freely and loosely at any other time its intention is to manipulate us into supporting their Manichean view of the world. Some political theorists argue that politics cannot really function at all unless there is an identifiable enemy to point the finger at. Without it, politicians have trouble rallying support to themselves. Robert Cooper, the diplomat and former foreign-policy adviser to Tony Blair, has suggested it is no coincidence that the War on Terror came along so soon after the Cold War, which had divided us into two camps, was over.

Once the manipulative language has caught on and becomes the accepted way of talking about complex issues, it becomes difficult to break out of it. Anyone who tries risks a pretty sharp, accusatory response that carries with it the implicit charge of treachery. 'Oh, so you don't think 9/11 was enough evidence that they've declared a war of terror on us? You don't think Saddam Hussein was an evil dictator? Is that really what you're saying?'

There is a word for this sort of thing: hysteria. The manipulation of language is one of the surest ways of generating it.

George Bush said the world 'had never seen such a crime as 9/11'. Why, I wonder, do politicians feel the need to exaggerate even such terrible acts? Why can they not let the atrocity speak for itself? Everyone knows there have been 'such crimes' – crimes on a vastly greater scale of magnitude. What was the Holocaust or Stalin's terrors or Mao's mass murders? Bush also said, 'We will rid the world of evil-doers.' The absurdity of such language scarcely needs pointing up.

Operation Infinitely Misleading

The overworked notion of truth being the first casualty of war does not describe precisely enough what happens. It is not just that the chaotic events of war often make it impossible to report accurately, or that each side tells lies to mislead the enemy deliberately. It is often the case that the meaning of words is abandoned altogether.

Think of the euphemisms of war: collateral damage; the degrading of assets; smart bombs; surgical strikes; humane war. Think, too, of the official names given to military operations. The one used for the aerial assaults on Baghdad in 2003 was unusually honest: 'Shock and Awe'. Others are less so.

The Israelis attacked the Rafah refugee camp in 2004, bulldozing many homes with virtually no warning and with many people still in them. It was called 'Operation Rainbow'. When the US Marines blasted the town of Fallujah after some American contractors were murdered they called it 'Operation Vigilant Resolve'. Their resolve gave way under a strong defence by the insurgents and they backed off.

The original name for the invasion of Afghanistan was to be 'Operation Infinite Justice'. This was changed after it was pointed out that Muslims believe that only Allah – and not American helicopter gunships – is capable of delivering infinite justice. They changed it to 'Enduring Freedom'.

Acronyms are useful to present a sanitised version of horror. Justin Marozzi was impressed with some he learned when he worked in Baghdad after the war. The one he disliked most was VBIED. It stands for Vehicle Borne Improvised Explosive Device. It means a car bomb.

Words of Mass Deception?

And think, too, of WMD – an acronym that must surely be tattooed by now on the inside of some politicians' brains. The phrase 'weapons of mass destruction' has been around for a long time, even if it did not impinge on the consciousness of most of us until the months before the Iraq war. Until then its meaning had been pretty closely defined: long-range nuclear, chemical or biological weapons used against large populations. All those characteristics had to exist to justify the description, though some experts have always felt chemical weapons should not be included.

No one said Britain deployed WMD in the bombing raids on Dresden in 1945 even though tens of thousands of people were killed and long-range bombers were used. The weapons themselves were conventional high explosives – not 'WMD'. Nor were the battlefield nuclear weapons that were deployed during the Cold War. They had a short range and were not targeted on civilian populations. Indeed, no one outside defence ministries and intelligence agencies talked about WMD at all. We didn't even know what the acronym meant until the dossiers were published to persuade us that Saddam Hussein was a threat who must be dealt with.

Millions of words have been written about why we went to war in Iraq and whether it was the right thing to do. This book is concerned with language – and the way words were manipulated by all sides throughout those months is an object lesson. WMD made a gradual transition from being long-range weapons that threatened mass destruction and could be deployed within forty-five minutes to battlefield weapons that might or might not have been available for use at short notice. In the event, as the world knows, they did not exist – or if they did, they were never found. Instead of gleaming missiles loaded with deadly warheads, the search shifted, in George Bush's words, to 'WMD programme-related activities'. There are several possible explanations for what happened. One is that the politicians were misled by faulty intelligence. Another is that words were manipulated to influence attitudes. Whatever the truth, language is a powerful weapon in its own right.

The Nobel Laureate Wole Soyinka said this in his 2004 Reith Lectures about WMD:

> It was a sustained demonstration, both as metaphor and as prophecy, of how empty such rhetoric can prove, yet how effectively it can blind the people, lead them into a cul-de-sac, securing nearly an entire nation within a common purpose that proves wrongly premised. Outside that nation itself more than a few others were swept up in the hysteria that was stimulated by no more than this simple but passionate evocation of that mantra, 'weapons of mass destruction'.

It might be worth remembering that the weapons that kill most people are not WMD at all, but the humble AK 47 and similar guns, which can be bought for a few pounds in most third-world countries.

Language Lite

For all their love of 'war' as a metaphor, politicians tend to shun it in times of real crisis, when soldiers may be sent to risk their lives. Most of us have seen it only on television and what we see is sanitised war. We watch the soldier firing a weapon and we do not see the bullet smash into flesh or the piece of shrapnel ripping off an arm or a leg.

But many people know the reality. They have lost family and friends on a foreign battlefield or seen their homes destroyed in the Blitz or come home from war disabled and disfigured. So the politicians often seek a euphemism. They usually call it 'conflict' or 'combat'. There is something almost noble about the notion of combat, but those who have seen the real thing at first hand know there is nothing noble about war.

In 'conventional' war prisoners have the protection of the Geneva Conventions. In the new language of war it is different. President Bush's national security adviser, Condoleezza Rice, says the war on terror is 'a different kind of war'. Instead of POWs there are 'unlawful combatants'. They qualify for none of the protection and can be locked away in Guantanamo Bay for years without a charge being laid against them or access to a lawyer. Some go to other countries where their treatment may be even harsher. The term used to describe this process of surrendering suspects to other countries is 'rendition'. It involves, according to Congressman Edward Markey, 'our country out-sourcing interrogation to countries that are known to practise torture'. It is something, he said, that nobody wants to talk about. It helps to have an unfamiliar word such as 'rendition' to describe it.

I came across a new word for the treatment of

prisoners when I interviewed General Janis Kaplin-sky, the American soldier who was put in charge of all the prisons in Iraq in 2003. She was suspended from her command when details began to emerge of the way some of her prisoners were being treated. She told me that the commander of Guantanamo had been sent to Iraq to order it. The term for it was 'Gitmo-ise'. She said it was an acronym for Guantanamo Intelligence Treatment Methods. Put simply, she said, it meant 'Treat them like dogs.'

Even torture has its euphemisms. 'Enhanced interrogation techniques' is one. Another chilling phrase was offered by Wayne Madson, a former US Navy intelligence officer. He said the treatment was known as 'torture lite'. So we come full circle: the language of politics buys in from the language of consumerism. If we can get beer 'lite' then why not torture – or anything else? The writer Michael Ignatieff calls the twenty-first-century American imperium 'empire lite'.

There is an inevitability about all this. The more politics treats us as consumers rather than citizens, the more the language used will be the language of the marketplace. It must surely have reached its apogee with 'torture lite'. Hans Blix, once the United Nations' chief weapons inspector, said that when Bush and Blair persuaded us to go to war against Iraq they did not try to convince us with argument. They behaved, he said, 'like salesmen'.

When Henry Kissinger, the architect of the bombing of Cambodia, was awarded the Noble Peace Prize, the satirist Tom Lehrer said satire had become obsolete. He left the stage soon afterwards and went back to teaching. I wonder what he would have thought of some of the comments made when the war in Iraq was over. Paul Bremer was put in charge of the country by President Bush and he had this to say about the insurgents who were trying to end the American occupation:

> 'They think that power in Iraq should come out of the barrel of a gun. That's intolerable . . .'

And President Bush himself made this observation to an interviewer on Al Arabiya Television:

> 'Iraqis are sick of foreign people coming into their country . . .'

When politicians are unable to see the irony of their own words you begin to wonder whether it is not just we who become ensnared by the manipulative bewitchment of their language but they themselves. Or, as Robert Burns put it:

> O wad some Power the giftie gie us
> To see oursels as ithers see us!

No Rant . . .

We have that gift already – and it is called language. It's a question of how we use it. In this book I have tried to look at how we speak and write English and how it may be used to manipulate us. The best defence against the manipulators is to know what is going on. That is why we should demand that people in power use clear, simple English instead of the clichéd, dumbed-down, inflated and bogus management-speak that so often passes for English today. Yet this is the age of the visual image.

I wrote earlier that none of us who saw the pictures of the planes crashing into the Twin Towers will ever forget them – but I doubt that we can remember the words used to describe the horror. Some terrible things have happened in Iraq before and since the war, and many words have been written attacking the behaviour of the occupying forces and the insurgents. But did any of them do a fraction of the damage caused by that single picture of a prisoner being dragged like a dog on a leash by a grinning GI? I doubt it. So are we wasting our time bothering with mere words?

The answer is no. Images are powerful, but they are also crude. We cannot conduct the dialogue demanded by free citizens in an open society by trading them. Politicians may try to sell themselves to us largely through images, but if we are to hold them to account we need words to challenge the images. This is why we need a common language and this is why it needs to be taught properly and monitored constantly. That is why you, dear reader, are not wasting your time if you write to the BBC (or anywhere else) and complain about bad English. And write again if your letter is ignored. But we have to decide what we mean by bad English.

Professor David Crystal is probably the most prolific writer on the English language. He is very much an 'anything goes' man: language evolves so let's not worry too much about splitting infinitives. He's right about that. What matters, he says, is that we have a standard English in which we can be understood by each other. He's right about that too, even though I would prefer the phrase 'common English' for the reasons I have tried to outline in this book. But I think intelligibility is setting the bar a bit low. The language needs to be as versatile, nuanced and adaptable as we can make it – not rudimentary and limited.

When someone uses 'disinterested' with no idea of its real sense, we still grasp what he is trying to say, but the value of the word has been destroyed.

When language is inflated the impact is lost.

When hackneyed phrases and whiskery clichés are

trotted out without a thought as to what they mean they end up meaning nothing.

When euphemism becomes the norm real dialogue becomes impossible.

Let me end with this thought:

'One should not aim at being possible to understand but at being impossible to misunderstand.'

It was the Roman rhetorician Marcus Fabius Quintilian who said that two thousand years ago. I'd be happy to see him working in any newsroom or government office today.